101 WAYS
TO MAKE GENERATIONS
X, Y AND ZOOMERS
HAPPY AT WORK

ISBN 978-0-9780363-2-4

National Library Cataloguing-in-Publication Data available on request from the publisher.

SYNTHESIS AT WORK INC
1000-355 BURRARD ST
VANCOUVER BC CANADA V6C 2G8

Editorial & production support by GF Murray Creative Info Solutions, Coquitlam BC

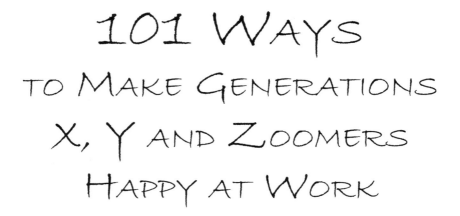

101 Ways
to Make Generations X, Y and Zoomers Happy at Work

by
Cheryl Cran

Synthesis at Work Inc
1000-355 Burrard St
Vancouver BC Canada V6C 2G8

ACKNOWLEDGEMENTS

This book would not have been written without my marketing manager Karen Harris and her team at CMI Speaker Management. Seriously, it is because of her that this book got written. I would like to thank the many clients who requested this book after downloading my free e-book *Five Ways to Lead the Generations* off of my web site.

Thanks to Arnold my book agent, Kedre my incredible editor, Dale Clarke for cover concept and Cathy for cover design.

And, once again, to Reg. This is the fourth book and your continued support means so much.

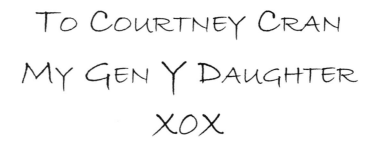

To Courtney Cran
My Gen Y Daughter
xox

1: INTRODUCTION

Why should we care whether Gen X, Y or Zoomers are happy at work?

See the press release below by the Conference Board on the decrease in job satisfaction among Americans.

PRESS RELEASE / NEWS

US Job Satisfaction at Lowest Level in Two Decades
Jan. 5, 2010

Americans of all ages and income brackets continue to grow increasingly unhappy at work—a long-term trend that should be a red flag to employers, according to a report released today by The Conference Board.

The report, based on a survey of 5000 US households conducted for The Conference Board by TNS, finds only 45 percent of those surveyed say they are satisfied with their jobs, down from 61.1 percent in 1987, the first year in which the survey was conducted.

"While one in ten Americans is now unemployed, their working compatriots of all ages and incomes continue to grow increasingly unhappy," says Lynn Franco, director of the Consumer Research Center of The Conference Board. "Through both economic boom and bust during the past two decades, our job satisfaction numbers have shown a consistent downward trend."

Fewer Americans are satisfied with all aspects of their employment, and no age or income group is immune. In fact, the youngest cohort of employees (those currently under age twenty-five) expresses the highest level of dissatisfaction ever recorded by the survey for that age group.

"The downward trend in job satisfaction could spell trouble for the overall engagement of US employees and ultimately employee productivity," adds Franco.

"These numbers do not bode well given the multi-generational dynamics of the labor force," says Linda Barrington, managing director, Human Capital, The Conference Board. "The newest federal statistics show that Baby Boomers will compose a quarter of the US workforce in eight years, and since 1987 we've watched them increasingly losing faith in the workplace." Twenty years ago, some 60 percent of that generation was satisfied with their jobs. Today, that figure is roughly 46 percent. Barrington adds: "The growing dissatisfaction across and between generations is important to address because it can directly impact the quality of multi-generational knowledge transfer—which is increasingly critical to effective workplace functioning."

The drop in job satisfaction between 1987 and 2009 covers all categories in the survey, from interest in work (down 18.9 percentage points) to job security (down 17.5 percentage points) and crosses all four of the key drivers of employee engagement: job design, organizational health, managerial quality, and extrinsic rewards.

"Challenging and meaningful work is vitally important to engaging American workers," adds John Gibbons, program director of employee engagement research and services at The Conference Board. "Widespread job dissatisfaction negatively affects employee behavior and retention, which can impact enterprise-level success." In fact, 22 percent of respondents said they don't expect to be in their current job in a year. "This data throws up a big red flag because the increasing dissatisfaction is not just a 'survivor syndrome' artifact of having co-workers and neighbors laid off in the recession," says Gibbons.

Source: Research Report #1459–09-RR The Conference Board, *I Can't Get No... Job Satisfaction, That Is: America's Unhappy Workers*

Read on to find 101 ways to make the generations happier at work, and perhaps your company can avoid the dramatic shift in employee behavior expected when the economy becomes robust once again.

2: About Gen X

Gen X wants meaningful work or to feel part of a meaningful workplace. Take Lain Hensley, for example. He has always had a passion for helping those in need. In 2001, he saw the opportunity to do that when he was hired by Lucent Technologies.

Part of his job was to help the supply chain team work together. Instead of running a typical training program, Lain had the Lucent employees work with the American Society for the Prevention of Cruelty to Animals to construct homes for dogs. The exercise was a huge success. Since then, they have built entire training programs around causes and helping others.

Generation X (those in their thirties to mid-forties) just happened to be coming into the workplace for the first time during the 1990s, when some of the most profound changes ever in the economy, society, culture, and the workplace were just starting.

This generation's views were shaped by the following influences during their formative years:
- ✓ Watergate
- ✓ MTV
- ✓ Fall of the Berlin Wall
- ✓ 18 percent interest rates in the late 1980s
- ✓ The 1990s recession
- ✓ Job insecurity

Businesses in the 1990s learned to be lean and flexible. A by-product of this was the prospect of frequent job layoffs—and less job security. The myth of a career with a single company was dead. This is why Gen X does not have the mentality of working for one employer until retirement.

Key trends during the 1990s included the tech boom, the dotcom boom, and a drop in unemployment levels, all of which were occurring as these new workers were getting their first tastes of real work experience.

Experienced businesses were looking at Gen Xs with fear in their eyes. They began to think that Gen Xs had figured out magical business models: that they could make money without providing services or product. But that was the myth of the new economy. People who thought the new economy was about dotcoms and magical business models were not paying attention. The real new economy (back then and right now) is about a highly interconnected, rapidly changing, fiercely competitive, knowledge-driven global marketplace in which needs become unpredictable. That means that staffing strategy has to change.

Let's spend a little time getting inside the head of Gen X.

- ✓ They are always looking for opportunities.
- ✓ They are not loyal to a company, but loyal to a manager.
- ✓ They view peers as competitors.
- ✓ Life comes first, work second.
- ✓ They are used to being downsized.
- ✓ They want an informal relationship with authority figures.
- ✓ They want a lot of attention, recognition, and back-patting.
- ✓ They feel they are the undervalued generation behind the Boomers.

The "lives first, work second" attitude is a key characteristic of Gen X. (They have this in common with Gen Y.) This group has younger families, older parents, and very high stress levels. Many Gen Xs have put off having a family until their mid- to late thirties, which is causing much stress in work environments in which Zoomers are the primary age group. Gen Xs produce high volumes of work and have strong commitment to their work, but once they make the family choice they want to be there for their children. They don't want to model the Zoomers, who were never home, thus causing Gen Xs to be latchkey kids.

Generation X is frustrated with their Zoomer leaders because they feel that Zoomers talk about work–life balances but aren't sincere. Gen X is also challenged by the apparent lack of movement from the Zoomers to use technological solutions. Gen X feels that Zoomers are fixed in their attitudes, and that their rigid rules are stifling productivity and profit.

Gen Xs fear that looking for life balance will jeopardize their careers with their Zoomer bosses. They feel that Zoomers sacrificed family for job security and advancement, and that they expect Gen X to do the same.

Gen X has shaped the real new economy. The difference between Generation X and everyone else in the 1990s was that Generation X never had it any other way. As their parents did, members of Generation X are growing up, buying houses, and raising families. They are the first generation to reach adulthood in the new economy, but as they mature they no longer want to spend a lifetime with one company as previous generations did. The conservative, security-seeking Zoomer is not the Gen X, who is neither security-driven nor stuck on a return to tradition. For Gen X it's about keeping your options open because you have to take care of your family. There is no turning back.

Tina Fey, former *Saturday Night Live* star and star/head writer for *30 Rock*, is a great example of an opportunity-grabbing Gen X. She models the ability of Gen Xs to always keep your eye out for a new opportunity even if you are really busy. She writes and acts for the Emmy, SAG and Golden Globe award-winning *30 Rock* but her uncanny resemblance to Sarah Palin provided a hot opportunity. When *Saturday Night Live* producer Lorne Michaels asked her to return to *SNL* as Sarah Palin during the presidential race in 2008, Fey jumped at the chance. And the rest, shall we say, is history.

So how can we make Gen X happy at work? Take a look at the workloads of Gen Xs. Provide them with the support that was taken away in the Zoomer work environment. This support may be in the form of improved or increased technology. Or increased training and clear succession planning.

Give more control to Gen X leaders, and provide them with the freedom to make entrepreneurial decisions in the workplace. One of Gen X's biggest complaints is that there are too many rules, too much structure and not enough creative license.

If it makes sense for your company, allow Gen X the flexibility to work from home. They will work their tails off and work well to performance measurements (rather than just nailing the clock-in time at the office).

Manage your expectations of the work output of Generation Xs, especially if you are a Zoomer leader. Provide flexibility while still demanding high standards.

Gen Xs are far more adaptable to change than Zoomers generally. Involve your Gen Xs in leading change.

Customize your rewards and recognitions to match the individual needs of each of your Gen Xs. Give some thought to meaningful and personalized recognition.

Provide *à la carte* benefit options so that each Gen X gets his or her needs met. (For example, provide pet leave for bereaved pet owners as an option for those who do not have children.)

Groom them for executive and high leadership positions or risk losing them when they go to start their own businesses.

Welcome their ideas, and give them the opportunity to run with their ideas.

Of course, you don't have to do any of these things, but if you don't you risk losing your valuable Gen X talent either to the competition or to funnelling their entrepreneurial energy into their own businesses. As an illustration, a well-known talent agency in North America had a Gen X superstar on its sales team. She epitomized Gen X attributes: she worked hard and was motivated by results for efforts. She requested the opportunity to work from home for two days a week due to family changes. At first the request was denied because company policy was that all sales staff had to work in the bullpen. This tenacious Gen X continued to ask for flexibility, and finally the company relented by giving her one day a week at home.

Her numbers went up, her productivity wasn't hampered and her clients were happier than ever. However, the company felt she wasn't part of the team, so she started to get pushback again when she asked for two days a week at home. This company chose to stick to its model of the last twenty years instead of looking at innovative ways to manage a team that works partly in the office and partly from home. The ability to make it work was there but the company chose to stick to the rules. In the end the Gen X quit and is now happily applying her natural entrepreneurial tendencies to working as an outsourced sales professional.

Zoomers are still very attached to structure, form and rules, and this will create further divides with Gen X workers as they strive to work in ways that suit them and yet still produce results. Gen Xs are not afraid to lose their jobs; they expect job volatility. They are more afraid of boredom, lack of creativity and rigidity around structure.

3: About Gen Y

Fast Company magazine's February 2009 cover story was about snowboarding champ Shaun White, a Gen Y who epitomizes the values of his demographic: creativity and authenticity.

Twenty-two years old, with a passion for snowboarding and now a multi-millionaire, Shaun is a Gen Y who came from working-class roots with a love for snow. As Shaun has shown, when you put together hard work and natural ability, Gen Ys can absolutely rock the workplace with their energy, commitment and contributions.

The trend experts say that besides Shaun's natural athletic abilities, his business sense is based on friendship-building and authenticity. If there are two things Gen Yers can't stand it is insincerity and bullshit. Shaun's ability to turn his talent into a video game and capitalize on his appeal to his own demographic is a lesson to be learned by business owners and leaders.

Gen Yers will listen and respond to other Gen Yers. This is the Facebook, MySpace, Twitter and Second Life generation. This is the generation whose childhoods were so activity-based that they are bored silly in the workplace if they are not challenged, multitasking or being recognized for their contributions. This is the generation of our kids; we raised them this way and now they are showing up at work—and we don't know how to deal.

This generation's views were shaped by the following trends or happenings in their lifetime:

✓ Technology since birth
✓ Reality TV
✓ Zoomer divorce

- ✓ Multicultural classrooms
- ✓ Creativity taught in school
- ✓ Parents taught them to speak up
- ✓ Rewarded for just showing up
- ✓ Social networking (MSN, Facebook, MySpace, etc.)

Generation Y has seen their Zoomer and Gen X parents get downsized, divorced and re-married. Many have experienced blended families. They feel that their parents were not there for them.

This generation suffers a great deal of stress due to their scheduled lives and ongoing changes in the world. Because Generation Ys have lived through increased violence and global terrorism, their attitude is that life is precious, so they value family and friends deeply. Generation Ys are generally highly demonstrative and loving to their friends. They insist on life first; work is simply a convenient way of funding the life they want to live.

Let's get inside the head of Gen Y now.

- ✓ They want to connect and upon waking and will likely be text messaging their friends before they even get into the shower.
- ✓ They want to be significant and recognized for their contributions. (They were raised by parents who constantly told them, "You are wonderful. You can be and do anything.")
- ✓ They want to be famous—and YouTube and Facebook can make it happen.
- ✓ They think of work as a social opportunity to connect, brainstorm and work on projects.

They are not as motivated by money as the Zoomer or Gen Xs are; they are more motivated by perks such as time off, ski trips, and office fun activities (like Nintendo Wii). Unlike Zoomers, they want to make friends at work and enjoy after-work socializing. If they like the people they work with they want to hang with them outside of work too.

Here's an example of Gen Y not being motivated by money. Anita, a Gen Y manager that I have been coaching for fifteen months, has been working hard at her sales career in the recruiting industry. She started right out of college, and her personality is outgoing, driven and matter of fact. When she started with the recruiting company, her Gen

X owner/boss treated her with respect and gave her high expectations to perform. Anita became one of the top-selling salespeople in her group and was promoted to sales leader. Although Anita liked her sales job she wasn't overly sure she wanted to be a leader: it seemed like more work, less selling and likely more stress. Her boss convinced her that she was the right fit, though, and Anita took the job. I was hired to coach her in leadership skills. Sales skills are unique to selling; leadership skills are quite different.

Anita was doing such a fantastic job in both her sales role and her leadership role that the company gave her a trip for two to New York. They could have increased her compensation, but the boss knew this would only mildly motivate her. When Anita was given the trip she was over the moon. Anita took her husband and they had the time of their lives. That trip was three years ago. Anita still talks about it, remembers its impact, and values that the boss recognized her in that way. Since that trip Anita has been rewarded with many other travel-related perks, and she reports that this is far more appealing to her than a 3 percent raise. After all, she is in sales and she can earn more in commissions any day.

The average Gen Y will change jobs up to twenty times in his or her lifetime, whereas Traditionalists stayed with the same employer until retirement, Zoomers changed jobs approximately three to five times, and Gen X will change jobs five to ten times in their lifetimes.

Generation Ys were born into technology and grew up with it as part of life. Most Gen Ys have more than one TV and two computers per household. Their preferred communication method is instant messaging, and their preferred way of learning is through video games or computer games. This is quite different than the "lecture" style of learning that Zoomers and Gen Xers became accustomed to.

Gen Ys are not loyal to a company; instead, they are loyal to their friends. If they feel their bosses or co-workers are like friends they will stick around. If they dislike their boss they will quit with little concern.

On average Gen Y does not leave home until they are thirty-five years old! You might be thinking, not me—ours are away at college. Well, guess what? They are coming back! If a Gen Y is still living at home and a Zoomer or Gen X boss tells them to do something or they are fired, Gen Y has no survival issues. Why? Because they still have a roof over their head.

So how do you lead Gen Y?

Be up front with them. You know they want to learn as much and get as much from the company as they can before moving on.

Increase technology and knowledge of technology in the workplace. Gen Y expects to have the best technological tools available to them.

Give them what is important to them to get them to stay (such as paying for their education and providing social, fun activities) and support them as people.

Set them up with a guide who can support them to succeed. If Gen Ys feel they are failing, they will give up quickly and become apathetic.

Show them how their work affects overall company goals. How does what they do as people affect what the company does in the marketplace?

Involve them in a company charity event or environmental cause. Generation Y is the most humanitarian generation.

Allow them to have a life. Give flex days off, and be flexible with start and finish times.

Treat them as friends. Gen Ys will not automatically respect authority or leadership, because they feel respect is personally earned (not given based on a title).

As we move forward in the book we will dig deeper into the individual components of the workplace and how we can shift or change the rules that have been in place for the working lifetime of a Zoomer. With Gen Y in the mix, things aren't just changing, they are transforming.

4: About Zoomers

The term "Zoomer" was coined by Canadian Moses Znaimer (www. zoomermag.com), well known for his contrarian views on aging and modern Baby Boomers. In his estimation a Zoomer is a Baby Boomer who refuses to age.

Just a few years ago we were hearing about the crisis that employers would soon be facing because Zoomers were expected to retire. Of course, this was before the recession of 2008–2009. What the recession created for employers were layoffs and downsizing but for many of their Zoomer employees it created the necessity to work later in life than they had planned.

Mandatory retirement has been replaced with extended retirement. Progressive companies are recognizing that not only can they hold on to their Zoomer employees longer but also that they can work with them in a new and exciting way.

For the last ten years I have been predicting the "free agent nation" where people would be working more on contracts, with flex time and control over their work schedules. It turns out that the modern Zoomer really doesn't want to retire anyway. They want to continue to earn money while having the life that they want, in the free agent nation.

Take my friend Fanny Kiefer (www.shaw.ca/thefannykiefershow), who is in her early sixties and has absolutely no intention of retiring. Her local cable talk show has been in production for over ten years and she absolutely loves what she does. We had dinner a few months ago and she proclaimed that she will continue working until she drops dead while doing what she loves. I think that's the key distinction—Zoomers are now realizing that work does not have to be drudgery. It can be fulfilling and rewarding and therefore it is something we would want to continue doing indefinitely.

I had a conversation the other day with a sixty-one-year-old woman who owns her own business. She said that she plans to work until the day she dies. She sees her work as a way to stay connected and informed and it keeps her feeling alive.

So how do you make Zoomers happy at work?

It is important to remember that just because groups of people are in the same demographic does not mean that every person wants the same thing. We must look at people as individuals and we have to customize our solutions in a way that meets the most common preferences for the people we want to hire and keep.

Zoomers are looking for ways to continue working but want to work within their lifestyle. They want the option of working a certain number of days per week or they want the option of working on a contract.

All three generations want the opportunity to take a sabbatical to travel or study, or in the case of contract work, to have time between contracts for travel or study.

I predict that more employers will provide *à la carte* benefits and personal options to meet the customized needs of Zoomers.

For example, you could have four people, all at the age of forty-five, with the following life scenarios:

- ✓ Married with grown kids and now wants to travel with spouse
- ✓ Single with aging parents and responsible for their welfare
- ✓ Married for the second time with newborn or adopted child and wants stability
- ✓ In an alternative relationship and wants to go to Third World countries to volunteer.

Many Zoomers are afraid to teach what they know to Generation Xs because they are worried about job stability. It is important to coach and teach Zoomers to get comfortable with "downloading their knowledge" to their teams. Companies would benefit from offering incentives and rewards for Zoomers who download most effectively and who have built solid succession plans.

Zoomers love technology if it is easy to learn and makes their jobs easier. Typically Zoomers will resist technology if it does not make their jobs easier or if there is a long learning curve involved. Zoomers respect efficiency and appreciate it when their Gen X and Y colleagues can show them quick and easy ways to get something done.

5: FLEXIBILITY

A recent study released by the Conference Board of Canada states that the Zoomers (Baby Boomers who refuse to age), Gen X and Gen Y have more in common than we might think.

Each group makes inaccurate generalizations about the others and often these generalizations are negative. But when the question posed to all generations was, "What do you want in the workplace?" the answers were remarkably similar.

The list included respect, flexibility, fairness and the opportunity to do interesting and rewarding work. The report was based on a survey of 900 workers with even representation from each generation.

When I present interactive keynotes on generations in the workplace I focus on how each generation can recognize what their biases against other generations are, and work to bridge the communication gap.

The key is to build positive generalizations about each of the generations so that we can focus on their strengths and move forward to create more teamwork, more creativity and ultimately a more motivated workforce.

All generations have more in common than we believe and one of the commonalities is that all generations want similar things in the workplace. In the years that I have been speaking and consulting on communication and leadership I have found that employees are happiest and morale is highest when the work environment allows flexibility.

My daughter Courtney, now twenty-two, is going to school part time to get her psychology degree and also works part time in a restaurant as a server. Courtney has told me that she loves working in the hospitality industry because they understand what is important to people her age. She willingly works the shifts they give her but with enough notice she can get time off when she wants. Her boss knows she loves hockey and has taken her to a Canucks game. The restaurant works around her schedule at school because they support her desire to get her degree. What also appeals to Courtney is the amount of money she can make—she puts on a smile and provides good service because she knows that it directly affects her tips and revenue.

Many employers forget the power of incentives. Gen Y is especially motivated by flexibility: getting more time to live their lives.

What does flexibility look like to a typical Gen X? As I mentioned in Chapter Two, Gen Xs are in their thirties to early forties and are either starting families or have small children. Flexibility for a Gen X is having the ability to leave early or come in late so that they can be involved in what is going on with their kids. A consulting client of mine is in his early forties and he and his wife have two small children aged five and three. He is an entrepreneur with a business partner—his partner does not have a family yet. It has been a difficult transition for Peter because he is trying very hard to run the business to his partner's satisfaction while still being an attentive father. If a business owner or a boss does not understand or is unwilling to provide support to the Gen X with a family, the result is a very unhappy and ultimately an underperforming employee.

I have been coaching both partners in the business I've discussed above. One thing I notice is that the single Gen X partner has more energy, makes time to exercise and is intensely focused on the business. The married Gen X partner is struggling to maintain a balance between being a business partner and a husband and father. The solution is not simple and in this case we needed to sit down and discuss some solutions for Peter. One solution we came up with was that he needed to add exercise back into his life, even if it appeared that he didn't have the time.

Large organizations have known that exercise and well-being are important to their employees' happiness and performance. Some companies like Best Buy and Zappos even provide exercise opportunities in the workplace such as a basketball court or a gym.

In the case of Care Pest they have a gym membership incentive, which is great, but the challenge is then to build in the scheduling flexibility that allows employees to use the benefit. Recently I helped implement an employee survey in another company. The majority of the leaders there are Gen X. One of the comments I received was that the company was great at making options such as gym memberships available but that the employees didn't feel they could use them because of time expectations on the job.

Holistic companies such as Lululemon have noticed that by providing their employees with flexible opportunities to exercise, total sick days dropped by half and the individual productivity of employees who regularly exercised went up.

Ways to incorporate flexibility to make Gen X, Y and Z happy at work:

- ✓ Vacation flexibility in off-peak periods (if employees take off-peak vacation time they receive bonus time off or extra flex days)
- ✓ Work schedule flexibility or "flex time," which could include late starts and late finishes, earlier starts and earlier finishes or shortened lunch hours.
- ✓ Optional extra hours: for example, if someone wants to go for an hour's run they can build it into their day as part of their schedule.
- ✓ Performance-based work, so hours spent are less important than results.

The Winter Olympics in Vancouver BC in February 2010 posed interesting challenges for employers in the area. Best Buy Canada offered its employees Olympic options. One employee chose to go in to the office at five AM and go home by two PM to avoid the major travel times for Olympic visitors.

Other companies allowed their workers to work from home for the majority of the Olympics. Some offered special transportation, such as a bus to pick up employees from a central Skytrain station.

These are all examples of building on the realities of an employee's life to make it easier for them to come to work. I see this trend continuing as our global village shrinks and technology allows us to work from almost anywhere in the world.

6: CONTROL

In my book *The Control Freak Revolution* I talk about how important it is for leaders and teams to be able to take positive control of their work environments, their communication and how they interact with others.

The concept of control and making Gen X, Y and Z happy at work is really based on the psychology that the more control individuals have over choices, environment and work the happier they are and the more they can contribute.

Zappos is a great example of a company that allows its employees a lot of autonomy in controlling their work environments. I visited their head office when I was in Las Vegas in 2009 and I was very impressed by the creative freedom and expression that the Zappos culture allowed their employees.

The CEO at the time, Tony Hsieh (Zappos has since been sold to Amazon), is an incredible visionary who also happens to be a Gen X. He totally understood the concept of empowering his teams with control.

When I took Zappos' head office tour, each department we went by was decorated according to the team's choice and they would greet each visitor based on their theme. For example, the marketing department was decorated with Elvis memorabilia and when you walked by the team would say, "Thank you for visiting, thank you very much," and then they would continue working. Some even dressed up in Elvis wigs that they pulled out when they saw a tour coming to their department.

Another department (I think it was accounting) was decorated as a jungle—hmmm, that's interesting. The entire department, including the ceiling, was covered in greenery, complete with hanging monkeys that screamed at you when you walked by.

The HR department said that having each department decide on a theme as a team and then interacting with the theme during tours was a huge morale booster for team members. Not only that, the entire team would then tweet about their team, department or visitors, which further increased the fun and showed the pride they had in their department.

An uptight business owner or leader would not want to give employees this type of control for a variety of reasons, but quite frankly Gen X and Y are looking for fun and creativity in the workplace. It is no surprise that the average demographic in Zappos is Gen X and Y.

I have worked as a consultant with a number of companies in which the owners or CEOs have continued to do tasks that should have been delegated or empowered to their leadership team long ago. For example, the supervisor and/or the team leader normally posts the job, collects the résumés, interviews and recommends a candidate. The general manager sits in on the decision interview only. In a company with annual revenues of $3 million I found the CEO was still doing all of the hiring even though he had seven team leaders! I pointed out that his leaders were not taking full responsibility for their teams' success because they didn't have a sense of ownership with their people. In other words, employees were dropped into their departments without their input. They were supposed to manage them without ever having been involved in the hiring process.

How control can make Gen X, Y and Z happy at work:

✓ In what areas of the job and the workplace can you give more control to your employees: their work area, their hours, their team activities? Get creative!

✓ Conduct team meetings on the concept of positive control, which is focused on accountability and responsibility, but also on having fun.

✓ Use technology to give employees more control. Best Buy US has a variety of forums designed to give employees more control, such as the "Water Cooler" and "Blue Shirt Nation." These intranet forums allow the employees to gain knowledge from each other and then share and manage the information among themselves.

✓ When delegating, give up tasks that are fun. Let your team members work on the fun stuff rather than the mundane or boring tasks. Great leaders learn to empower their teams to think for themselves and to create their own solutions.

✓ Rotate your meeting leaders. Instead of controlling the agenda yourself let the members of your team take turns being in charge of the meeting: everything from setting up the agenda and getting team buy-in to taking action and following up.

7: EMPATHY

How does empathy make the generations happy at work?

Daniel Goleman, who originated the concept of emotional intelligence, believes empathy is a key trait in making great leaders with the ability to manage at very high levels.

The table below, excerpted from *Emotional Intelligence* by Daniel Goleman, shows the difference between handling a situation with empathy and without empathy.

	With empathy	Without empathy
Core relational skills	You project a caring attitude.	You risk being viewed as aloof, uncaring, selfish and conceited.
Insight into others	You appreciate the thoughts, beliefs, desires and outlook of others.	You ignore or guess at others' perspectives.
Problem solving/ decision making effectiveness	You look at the whole picture to understand how others will be affected.	You risk overlooking human impacts and missing out on valuable alternative solutions.
Collaborative effectiveness	You share differences in thought and mindset, which are vital to joint intellectual pursuits.	You don't often hear or consider differing thoughts or opinions without making negative judgments.
Presentation skills	You meet the needs of the majority of your audience.	You risk engaging only a small portion of your target audience.

A leader with high emotional intelligence tends to have greater team loyalty and team engagement. Employees feel safe in an environment that has leaders who foster a culture of empathy.

Gen Ys can develop empathy by understanding how hard the Zoomers have worked—even though the Zoomers' past is not Gen Y's reality.

Gen Xs can develop empathy by understanding Gen Y's approach to work and coaching them in the needs of the work environment while honouring their desire for play and fun.

Zoomers have become quite fixed in their attitudes around work and they would benefit from building empathy around Gen X's need to balance work with family. They also need to have empathy for the Gen Y who really does not understand how hard you, as a Zoomer, has had to work. It's just not their reality.

Empathy can help the generations to connect, understand each other better and see things from the other generations' perspective.

8: Life Experience

You may be a Zoomer who currently feels very frustrated with Gen Ys who seem to lack experience, common sense and a work ethic. This bias rears its ugly head quite often with Zoomers. I call it a bias because really experience is learning on the job, which comes with time. Common sense is something created by learning from what doesn't work, and work ethics are based on whether you believe you have to work harder or work smarter. In a presentation I gave to a large building center client I asked all of the Zoomers in the audience to tell me out loud their frustrations with Gen Y. Their responses were similar to what I commonly hear elsewhere:

- ✓ Gen Ys act as if they are entitled
- ✓ Gen Ys don't want to put in the time
- ✓ Gen Ys don't have any common sense
- ✓ Gen Ys don't work as hard as we have had to in the past.

Then I turned it around and asked the Gen Ys to rebut the comments made by the Zoomers. I got back what I hear 90 percent of the time when I do this:

- ✓ I grew up believing I could have whatever I wanted pretty much when I wanted it and *you* told me this.
- ✓ I have learned that technology can speed up most tasks and that if I can creatively find an easier way to do something then there is more time for the fun stuff.
- ✓ In school we were taught to solve problems as a group. No one has taken the time to teach me their so-called "common sense" so I am left to figure it out on my own.

✓ It's not that I don't want to work hard. It's that I don't want to waste time with the way you choose to do it. If I can come up with a more efficient way, why begrudge me?

You can see right away how these two generations bring different life experiences to the workplace. Then throw the Gen Xers into the mix—they see things a little differently from either of the other two.

✓ Gen X feels gypped by the Zoomers, who told them that as long as they worked hard they would get rewards like promotions. Now that the Zoomers aren't retiring as planned they feel trapped.
✓ Gen X feels a little resentful of the confidence and *joie de vivre* of the Gen Ys. They have been playing the Zoomers' game and they are burned out.
✓ Gen X brings on-the-job experience and schooling to the workplace but not the same level of technical knowledge as Gen Y. They find themselves having to bridge that experience gap.

The range of life experience among the generations is causing more disruption in the workplace than ever before. It is also costing money: organizations use a figure-it-out approach instead of a strategic approach that asks, "How can we maximize the different levels of work experience we have and use it to our advantage from a competitive standpoint?"

Let's take a look at the generations and their different skills and experiences to see how we could creatively use them to generate dynamic, progressive workplaces.

	Gen Y	Gen X	Zoomers
Skills/Experience	Tech savvy	Project focus	People skills
	Group learner	Independent	Self starter
	Creative	Strategic	Goal setter
	Friendly and open	Friendly but guarded	Professional with less personal disclosure
	Adaptive	Strategically adaptive	Adaptive if forced

You can see from the table that there isn't a superior skill or experience level specific to a single generation. In order to create a workplace where all of the generations are happy to work we need to be willing to provide the training they need to succeed and contribute to the team dynamic. For example, if you are a Zoomer with a new Gen Y hire you may remember when you interviewed them they answered your questions in the "right" way, with what you wanted to hear! Gen Ys are taught how to give a good job interview in both high school and college. You might then notice in a week or two that the Gen Y you hired doesn't know half of what they needed to know to do the job they had been hired for. Who is at fault?

Well, actually it is the Zoomer, who didn't use a more savvy mechanism to find out if the Gen Y had the skills necessary to do the job. So what do you do? Fire them? *No.* You provide them with training and skills in areas where there are gaps and you get better at interviewing. A great tool is to provide potential hires with case studies of real workplace situations. See how they answer—that tells you a lot about their skill levels. They say they know how to use Excel, so ask them to build you a spreadsheet. Leave them with a computer and come back to see how they did.

It is inevitable that with generational differences wide ranges of experience in the workplace will exist. We need to get clearer on what it is we are trying to accomplish and look at the "why" instead of taking a judgmental "what's wrong with you?" approach.

Life experience is crucial in terms of creating a great working experience. Equally crucial is managing different experience levels among the generations.

9: SHARING

"Share your toys!" This was a message many Traditionalist parents instilled in their toddlers. Somehow it went from that to "Play to win" and "Knock out your competition."

Although Zoomers have been slogging away in work environments where "Play to win" and "Knock out your competition" were solid goals in the '80s and '90s, such dogma does not hold a lot of allure for the Gen Ys entering the workforce.

Gen Ys expect sharing when they get to the workplace and they are not motivated by knocking someone else down so that they can win. They are more motivated by group focus on a goal or group achievement with individual recognition of outstanding efforts. They realize that competition exists but they see it more as "co-opetition" where an organization cooperates with its competitors while gaining market share.

Even though Gen Y has grown up on video games in which they fight and compete to win the game they get points for helping others and for saving the world.

All generations benefit from sharing in the workplace—specifically when it comes to the sharing of knowledge. Here is a list of sharing strategies that go a long way to creating a happy workplace:

- ✓ Sharing knowledge: generously "downloading" what you know to everyone on your team so that you raise the bar for the entire team, help them do their jobs better and gain skills.
- ✓ Sharing resources: cross-departmental sharing of technology, people, solutions and ideas.

- ✓ Sharing people: cross-training and sharing people keeps the company dynamic and evolving, and flattens the learning curve for all three generations.
- ✓ Sharing clients: often a client who buys from one department is a great client for another department. Nike and Best Buy are great examples of companies that effectively use this strategy.
- ✓ Sharing updates: using social media such as Twitter, Facebook or LinkedIn allows all employees to share what is going on within the company. It's also a constant connection tool to potential buyers and happy customers.

Some questions to ask yourself in regards to sharing in your workplace are:
- ✓ What could we share more often that would increase camaraderie and teamwork within our culture?
- ✓ What resources are we hoarding? (For example, does one department have access to information and resources that would significantly help another?)
- ✓ What can we do to share our people? How can we formalize cross-training and cross-departmental learning?
- ✓ Are we sharing positive messages via social media about our company?

Sharing isn't just a childhood concept anymore. It is something vital to creating workplaces where all of the generations want to work.

10: Got Your Back

Many leaders and workers practice CYA in the workplace. CYA ("cover your ass") is a symptom of work environments that want specific results but have systems in place that make the results difficult for workers to achieve. Workers come up with their own ways to achieve the objectives while practicing CYA to protect the illusion that they are doing it the way upper management wants them to do it. CYA is also a strategy used by leaders who are worried about losing their jobs. They take protective measures, making sure they look good and keeping themselves off the firing line.

It still happens in today's workplace, but in many organizations there is less and less tolerance for CYA. Progressive companies recognize that creating a safe environment where employees feel their leaders and teams "have their backs" is far more conducive to truth telling and integrity, resulting in happier employees.

Gen X and Y have low tolerances for CYA leaders regardless of the leader's generation. The saying, "People don't leave their jobs, they leave their leaders" is all too true for Gen X and Y.

Jen, a young part time server who worked for a neighborhood restaurant, really enjoyed her job because of the tight-knit staff, the community atmosphere and her hip Gen X bosses. When one of her bosses stole money from the restaurant and then proceeded to cover his butt by fiddling with the servers' receipts she blew a gasket! Jen wasn't afraid of losing her job by outing the boss but she was uncomfortable confronting the boss himself or telling on him. You see, Gen Ys do not as a rule feel comfortable ratting someone out. She was infuriated that someone she looked up to would steal in the first place, but then to try and cover it up by setting up his own staff? Well, that was just too much for Jen to keep quiet about. She was ready to quit until the general manager asked her what was going on, at which point she explained what she'd found out. The smart Gen X manager promptly fired Jen's boss and begged Jen to stay on.

Trust is a huge element for building a happy workplace and organizations are moving away from CYA to transparency and openness. Gen X and Y want this but Zoomers are not used to it. Zoomers come from the "see no evil" or "speak no evil" generation, and they fear repercussions that could get them fired or treated poorly by their bosses or peers. There are a number of ways to demonstrate that leaders have their teams' backs but here are a few to check off and see if you and your company are doing all you can do to show that you have a safe and supportive workplace.

- ✓ As a leader you ensure that your team members have all the tools they need to succeed. If they don't have what they need you make sure to get it for them.
- ✓ When training your new team members you set up very clear expectations for completing tasks, their performance and how they can succeed.
- ✓ When a customer, team member or another leader complains about one of your team members, you make a positive assumption that your team member did the best they could. You then search out the "why" and from there take steps to help resolve the situation while providing the team member with the skill set to avoid future challenges of a similar nature.
- ✓ You set clear guidelines to your team on how they are to treat each other, communicate with each other and support each other—you create a culture of sharing.
- ✓ You recognize sharing. For example, if a Zoomer spends time downloading what they know to a Gen X or Y in a generous way you reward and recognize them publicly, because what gets rewarded gets repeated.
- ✓ In your regular meetings (whether face to face, teleconference or web-based) you remind your teams that you are developing a sharing culture and give examples of who has done a great job of it recently.

As humans we may resist sharing because we feel we are not getting back what we are giving out, but in the work environment—as in life in general—the adage "what goes around comes around" is true.

I feel that more and more companies are moving to truthful and transparent work environments as more and more of the workforce have low tolerance for lies and deception. Think of Enron and the financial collapse of 2008 (of course, there were a lot of corporate collapses due to lack of transparency prior to the Enron incident) and we can at least partially attribute the collapse and breakdowns to lack of ethics, truth and sharing.

11: CREATIVITY

Gen Ys are highly creative. Creativity is something that they have had access to since they were little kids. Just think about it—when most Zoomers were growing up they were taught reading, writing and math with very little emphasis on art. If they did take art, the classes were viewed as non-academic or unimportant. In contrast, Gen Ys were provided with many creative outlets by their Gen X or Zoomer parents. Those in the Gen Y group view the arts positively.

When my daughter Courtney was in grade three, her teacher was an avid follower of the arts. He placed a lot of emphasis on creativity, and because of this Courtney always loved art. Her teacher even asked for one of her paintings to keep because he felt she was so talented. That made a lasting impression on Courtney, who is now twenty-two. To this day she paints and writes poetry and credits her teacher for his influence.

The creativity of Gen Ys and their younger counterparts the Millenials is very exciting and encouraging, because clearly creativity is required as we move forward in a fast changing world with increased technology.

Progressive companies are recognizing that they have an opportunity to use Gen Y's natural creative abilities to help solve ongoing challenges in the workplace. An article posted on the news site Voxy.co.nz talks about New Zealand's Gen Ys as creative agents of change and credits them with showing more loyalty during the recession of 2008–2009:

New Zealand's Generation Y employees have changed from being demanding and unrealistic into creative agents of change, say participants at a CFO roundtable hosted by financial recruitment specialists Robert Half.

Chief financial officers and finance directors said younger employees had changed their attitudes during the recession—and their employers now saw them in a different light.

Just twelve months ago, employers were complaining about Gen Y's high expectations and lack of loyalty, saying twenty-somethings frequently changed jobs after six months to a year and expected rapid promotion and high salaries.

But now employers see engaged young people, able to think laterally and find creative solutions to pressing business problems.

"I see these people have converted from a drain into a resource, because they are staying longer," said Paul Chambers, former CFO of Transfield—now CFO of Meridian Energy. "They pick up enough of the business to work more effectively."

And they also refuse to unthinkingly accept established ways of doing things, which helps organizations that have to come up with smarter, more efficient ways of operating.

"They ask questions about why—why do we do it this way?" said Marlon Bridge, CFO of Manukau Water.

Those questions often led to different and more efficient ways of doing things, said Gary Agnew, CFO of electronic transactions company Paymark.

"None of the Gen Ys at Paymark have gone through a recessionary time before," he said. "They have taken on the challenge of looking at new and more efficient ways of doing things and saving costs."

Megan Alexander, general manager of Robert Half New Zealand, confirmed a change in attitude and said young job seekers no longer had unrealistic salary expectations. Also, because there were fewer jobs available, and fewer of their friends were changing jobs, they were happy to stay put for longer.

During the round table discussion, chaired by Robert Half Asia Pacific managing director David Jones, the finance leaders discussed how their organizations had adapted to the recession and how they were positioning themselves for the upturn.

All said the recession had brought an increased emphasis on loyalty—among businesses and their suppliers and customers, and also between businesses and their staff.

Grant Judge, head of finance and engineering for Downer Engineering, had a warning for the employers that had imposed pay cuts on their staff in the past twelve months: "As soon as there's a pickup, a lot of their people will change jobs."

And Megan Alexander had a word of caution for employers that had cut staff numbers but expected the same output from those remaining. "A lot of candidates are groaning under the pressure of heavy workloads," she said. Some were already beginning to look for new jobs, even though they realized their search might take several months.

"The opportunity for business in harnessing the creativity of Gen Y is to include them in high level discussions, ask for their input on long-standing challenges, gain insight on how to use technology more efficiently to get the results and provide a work environment that rewards creativity."

Gen X and Zoomers are creative as well, but not as innately as the Gen Ys because of their home and school environments in their formative years. All three generations tend to be happier and more likely to stick around in a workplace that honors creativity over strict and rigid processes.

Take a look at your systems and the way your company makes decisions. Perhaps there is an opportunity to bring more creativity into the workplace. Here are a few suggestions to help:

- ✓ Have creative solution contests using different media. For example, have teams or departments submit videos on what they think are a solution to a company concern.
- ✓ Reward creative ideas by giving sizable prizes to those who come up with good solid ideas. Many companies still have a version of the suggestion box, but in today's environment the suggestions aren't ignored—they are shared and explored.
- ✓ When holding meetings, allow a period of time (either as an icebreaker or during the meeting) for teams to do a creative activity.

Creativity will be the competitive edge in the next decade and Gen Y is a natural resource for companies to draw on.

12: STRENGTHS

Every generation has its own strengths and we need to consider how we can tap into the strengths of each of the generations in the workplace. In the book *Strengthsfinders 2.0* by Tom Rath the focus on finding people's strengths. It is an invaluable tool for scoping out people's individual strengths, but in this section I want to talk about the specific strengths characterizing each of the generations and how we can use that information to focus our goals, tasks and strategies.

If we shift our mindset from "each generation has a problem" to "each generation has innate strengths based on the lens with which they view the world" we can effectively leverage the skills of the people we have on board.

When I speak to groups about the generations I always ask what irritates them about other generations, but then I also ask what they appreciate about them. Here is what people see as Gen Y strengths:

✓ Peer oriented: they have a large network of resources and contacts
✓ Social media savvy: instant messaging equals instant answers and fast access to information
✓ Dream big: they are motivated by big dreams or visions because of the chance of gaining great recognition (shows like *American Idol* have made it seem that anyone can be a star)
✓ Give big: this group volunteers more than any other demographic and they believe they can make a big difference in the world
✓ Technically savvy: hand a Gen Y your iPhone and you end up with apps you never knew existed

✓ Big causes: Gen Ys want to be a part of something big. Big contribution, big recognition and big opportunities.

As I write this, the 2010 Olympics are literally in my backyard. My husband and I moved from the suburbs to Vancouver and our new place is smack dab in the middle of the Yaletown action. What has struck my husband and me is how patriotic the Gen Ys are! When you see crowd shots on TV or when we go for a walk among the massive Olympic crowds we see thousands of young people screaming "Go Canada Go" and just beaming with pride in their country. The media has stated they cannot believe the record number of people out participating and the majority is Gen Y. Why? Because they want to be part of something big and memorable. They want to be able to say they were part of a once-in-a-lifetime experience. If your company and you as a leader could create a work environment that focuses on the impact your products or services make on the world and how each person's contributions are building something bigger than themselves, then I promise you will engage and retain this generation. They will willingly share their strengths.

Let's look at the strengths of Gen X in the workplace and how they contribute to workplace success.

William Strauss and Neil Howe, co-authors of *Generations*, contend that each generation makes a unique bequest to those that follow and generally seeks to correct the excesses of the previous generation. They argue that the Zoomers went overboard on idealism and that the Generation X reaction to that excess involves an emphasis on pragmatism and effectiveness.

Gen Xers will be the leaders we need. Here are the Gen X strengths:

✓ Resourceful and hardworking: a latchkey childhood has made them take commitments and employability seriously.
✓ Self-reliance and strong survival skills: witnessing the lay-offs of the '80s has prompted a distrust of institutions. They have developed the ability to handle whatever comes their way with resilience. Xers instinctively maintain a well-nurtured portfolio of career options and networks.
✓ Operate comfortably in a global and digital world: many are avid adopters of the collaborative technology that promises to re-shape how we work and live.

✓ Global awareness: richly multicultural, they bring a more unconscious acceptance of diversity than any preceding generation.

✓ Innovation and looking for a different way forward: their strongest financial success as a generation has come from their entrepreneurial approach and achievements.

✓ Rich humor, healthy skepticism and the ability to isolate practical truths: help us all redefine issues and question reality.

✓ Fiercely dedicated to being good parents: because of their childhood they raise important questions about the way we all balance work with commitments beyond the corporation.

✓ Practical, value-oriented: effective stewards of both today's organizations and tomorrow's world.

You can see that the Gen X strengths are a great balance to the strengths of Gen Y. Let's look now at the strengths of the Zoomers, or Gen Z.

Generation Z, also known as the Zoomers, have strengths that have been developed over time and were shaped by their Traditionalist parents. The Zoomers grew up with the belief that you only got ahead with hard work. Their Traditionalist parents certainly worked very hard, typically in labor or blue-collar jobs, and often would leave the house in the early hours to work and not return until late at night. The Zoomers definitely modeled their work ethic after their parents.

The strengths of Zoomers are:

✓ "Put in the hours" work ethic: willing to work way beyond the standard eight hours.

✓ Commitment to get the job done: they grew up with the mottos "If you are going to do something do it right" and "Stay put until the job is done."

✓ Task-oriented: in fact, it makes them feel as if they are accomplishing something. They will often do mundane tasks even if they are not enjoyable.

✓ Willingness to take the lead: they were taught that leaders gain great recognition and that getting a promotion to leader means they are doing a good job.

✓ Follow through on deadlines and schedules: their professional environment values honoring promises made and doing what you said you would do.

✓ Great "professional" skills learned on the job: how to approach a client and how to follow protocol with higher-ups.

✓ On-the-job experience: this is something that can only be gained by putting in the years, which they have done willingly.

✓ Strong sense of loyalty: typically they will hang around longer than a Gen X or Gen Y due to an internal belief that they must try to make something work before they give up.

As you can see, each generation has great strengths. Based on these strengths we can look at which generation is best suited to certain projects or activities. Preferably as leaders we create teams incorporating members of each generation so that the mindsets and skill sets that each generation brings to the table can be used most effectively.

13: PERSONALITIES

I have shared with hundreds of audiences the merits of understanding personality types for increased communication effectiveness. In my consulting and coaching sessions, reviewing personality types is a key exercise before we start building strategies to move forward.

Here we are talking about generational differences and yet we know that we cannot put people into neat little boxes and label them based on generation, gender or personality. I think it is fair to say, though, that there are common threads that differentiate each of the generations that we can say are more true than false. For example, we can say that more women are focused on relationships and that more men are focused on results. It is fair to also say that certain personalities are more geared toward certain behaviors than others.

When I consult with organizations I encourage them to look at the whole picture of a person and their team so that we can deepen our understanding about who they are and what motivates them to results. Knowing your team member is a Gen Y female gives you some insight into what her values might be, but finding out her personality type gives you a more rounded picture. Many types of personality identification programs are available, such as Myers-Briggs, Kolbe, SELF and DISC, and they are all effective tools.

I took the components of each of the personalities and simplified them to what I call the Four Ds: Driver, Dancer, Detailer and Deflector. Understanding the personality piece of the puzzle is really helpful when you are working on having your team get along better and aligning their focus to allow you all to move forward.

Driver: Do It and Do It Now	Dancer: Do It and Have Fun
Moves and talks fast	Moves and talks fast
Fast decisions	Likes to socialize
No small talk	Smiles a lot, tells jokes
Business first	Great starter, not so good at finishing
No time for niceties	Likes to gossip
Results oriented	Wants to be recognized loudly
"Show me the money"	"Take me for lunch or coffee"
"Help me save time"	"Help me look good"

Detailer: Do It and Do It Right	Deflector: Can We All Get Along?
Moves and talks methodically	Measures what they say
Well thought out decisions	Procrastinates about decisions
Reserved and pensive	Friendly and uses a lot of words
Perfectionist	Cares what people think of them
Needs all the facts and proof	Doesn't want to hurt others' feelings
Likes research, in writing	Likes to be given choices
Uses words like "thought through, researched, took the time to go over…"	Reassure them and help them make a decision for less stress
"Take time to be thorough and understand my need for detail"	Show interest and concern for them

A quick exercise you can do with your team is to present the table above and ask them to review it. Then get them to select the personality style that they think least describes themselves. Ask them to put the number four in that box. Typically the primary or number one personality style is the one diagonally opposite to their number four. For example, I am least like a Deflector so my primary is Driver. Then ask them to intuitively choose their number two and three so that they have the styles in order from one to four. It is important to recognize that we all have all four styles operating in ourselves; however, we will typically show our top two styles (e.g. Dancer–Deflector) the majority of the time.

As you can see, your employee could be a Gen Y Driver–Dancer female, which now gives you all sorts of data to help you understand her better.

This is an invaluable tool for leaders and teams to help bring the generations together and help them understand that people aren't purposely trying to irritate them! Everyone has a unique personality, they come from a unique generation and they view the world through an individual lens.

14: Leadership

If there is one area in the work environment that we can focus on to make everyone happy it would be leadership.

I have lost count of the number of times that I have said that people don't leave their jobs, they leave their leaders. Each of the generations expects and wants different things from their leaders and although leaders cannot possibly be all things to all people they do need to adapt to diverse personalities.

Let's take a look at what each generation appreciates in a leader and what type of leader they would be happiest to work for.

Gen Ys are looking for friendly, approachable leaders who are willing to teach. They respond to "on the level" people who are real and who want to help others succeed. Gen Y struggles with reporting structures and protocols, and lack what a Zoomer might call "professional awareness." In their school environment Gen Ys were encouraged to speak to their teachers almost as peers, and they became comfortable going directly to an information source regardless of the person's status. Zoomer leaders may get frustrated by this because in the workplace Gen Y employees may appear as if they are going behind their backs when in fact Gen Y is simply going to the source without thinking about reporting structure. The Zoomer or Gen X leader needs to coach the Gen Y on the merits of reporting structure and provide reasons why it is part of corporate culture.

The leaders who do well with Gen Y are those who do not see them as a threat but rather as a young and creative group who can add value. The leaders who struggle with Gen Y are those who try to impose their values or expectations onto Gen Y without providing context or the information they need to succeed.

A seminar I conducted a few years ago for a utilities tech company had a leader who understood and adapted to his Gen Y employees with quite a bit of success. He decided that he would run his department of mostly twenty-somethings with a low structure, high outcome approach. He set up rotating work cycles and then had the Gen Ys sort out among themselves each week who would take which cycle. For example, if there was a big project in the works each component of the project was assigned a time block of four hours per day. The team had to ensure they met the project objectives set for those four hours and then report it for the next cycle. The four-hour cycle turned out to be highly effective—Gen Y tends to get bored quickly and easily. By setting up rotating projects with shorter time cycles and clear objectives the Gen Ys remained energized and eager to get the overall project done.

The leader also decided that their dress code could be casual since the team did not interact directly with the customers and, yes, tattoos and piercings were okay too.

Obviously this approach wouldn't work for every industry, but because the leader was willing to adapt to the Gen Ys on his team he created a highly engaged and results-oriented group.

A consulting of client of mine recently implemented instant messaging (IM) in his company when I told his leaders that Gen Y sees IM as efficient and e-mail as ancient history. As soon as they implemented the change their productivity soared, training opportunities increased and morale in the office went up.

Gen Xers have different needs from their leaders and feel frustrated with their Zoomer bosses. Gen X is the generation that lived through downsizing, restructuring and layoffs as a regular part of its work life and so its tolerance of poor leadership is quite low. In fact, I read in USA Today that more Gen Xers than any other demographic are starting businesses or leaving corporate life out of frustration with Zoomer leadership and lack of opportunity for promotions.

Gen Xs are looking for leaders who are generous with what they know and are willing to help the Gen X succeed, look good and get promoted. Gen X views many Zoomer leaders as information hoarders and this frustrates the heck out of them. Zoomer leaders will have great success with a Gen X if they view them as partners in their success, and keep an eye out for opportunities to recognize and promote them.

A great strategy for a Zoomer leader with Gen X is to let them have the publicity or bragging rights to successful projects. A self-assured Zoomer leader knows that they don't have to take the credit and that by giving credit to their hardworking Gen Xs they will increase loyalty and job happiness. It reminds me of Lisa, a co-worker of mine years ago when I was in the finance industry. She left to work for a large competitor. I heard from her about a year after she left and she was absolutely ecstatic about her boss. When I asked her why, she said her boss had been asked by a major human resources publication to be featured as an expert—and instead of taking it for herself the leader gave the opportunity to Lisa. Well, of course, Lisa was over the moon and her boss created a loyal, hardworking employee.

Gen X is also looking for Zoomer leaders who are willing to provide time off for family. Many Zoomer leaders resent this because they did not get the same benefit but Gen X is committed to balancing family with work and will soon become demotivated and look for work elsewhere if their Zoomer bosses do not provide them with family time.

The Zoomer employee is looking for much of what both Gen Y and Gen X are looking for but they are also looking for changes in how they do their work. The Zoomer worker has a "been there, done that" attitude and can be quite cynical if they do not have a leader who keeps things fresh for them, challenges them and provides them with opportunities to learn new things.

Zoomers are also looking for leaders who are hands-off. They want to be provided with guidelines and then they want to run with it. Unlike Gen Y, who wants to be given full and detailed information on how to do something, the Zoomer is looking for overviews and directions to resources.

Many Zoomers are not ready to retire or are delaying their retirement so they are looking for alternate work arrangements such as three days a week or part-time work, project-based work, extended vacations or sabbaticals.

In day-to-day office activities the Zoomer looks for a leader who is approachable, open to share what they know and inspires them to continue to learn and grow.

15: Motivation

No one can really make anyone do anything; however, we can inspire others to take action, to change and to do things differently. In today's workplace leaders need to be creative and adaptive to keep team members motivated. A great example is again Zappos, which I wrote about earlier. Their HR leader recognizes the importance of environment for motivation and allows teams the freedom to decorate their work areas. More than that, they encourage each of their employees to come up with creative Tweets and to be the face of the brand out there in cyber-land. Creativity is rewarded, resulting in increased motivation for everyone.

We are all human beings so there are some things that motivate all of us, but there are certain things that hold more motivational interest for each of the generations specifically.

Generation Y is the generation that was bribed by their parents to do things or have had their parents do things for them. In many ways their Gen X or Zoomer parents have indulged them so they haven't really had to develop internal motivation. This makes it challenging for leaders, because the tried-and-true "do this and you will get that" approach does not necessarily work for Gen Y. Zoomers and Gen X are easily motivated this way because they consider money important, but with Gen Y if you say, "Do this or you're fired," they say, "Okay, so fire me."

Threats or fear get you nowhere with a Gen Y. Such tactics work quite well with many Zoomers and Gen Xs, who have real-life financial concerns keeping them in check.

Gen Ys are motivated by:

✓ Personable and easy-to-relate-to leadership. They want to feel good around you.

- ✓ Easy money. They don't want to work as hard to earn money so if you can set it up so it seems they are getting easy money they will totally buy in.
- ✓ Team activities, such as group Nintendo Wii games, or going out as a company to a sports event or concert.
- ✓ Recognition in the form of perks, such as tickets to events or gift certificates for name brands.
- ✓ Altruism or philanthropy. If your company is giving back to society Gen Ys want to be a part of a bigger contribution.
- ✓ Environmental improvements. Green projects are motivating and inspiring.

As mentioned earlier in the book Gen Xs are in their thirties. They are starting families or have young families. They work hard while they are at work but they also want to get off work at a decent time, the flexibility to build in family activities and the freedom to work from home occasionally. Gen X is motivated by time off, big projects that earn them recognition and variety on the job. Here are some other ways to motivate Gen X:

- ✓ Money and time. If you can provide time-off incentives without affecting pay in a negative way Gen X would love this.
- ✓ Benefits choices. While many Gen Xs are having families there are also Gen Xs in alternative relationships or dealing with aging parents. They want flexibility around their benefit programs.
- ✓ Generous leaders who are eager to share what they know and who are willing to provide recognition and reward.
- ✓ Projects with a defined outcome and timeline. They prefer to focus on projects versus tedious task-oriented daily work.
- ✓ The option to work from home or out of the office on a regular basis. Even allowing Gen X one day a week to work from home can make them happier.
- ✓ Incentive to make money based on results, not "time on job." Gen X really does well in a performance-based workplace.

Zoomers are a little more cynical when it comes to motivation. This is the group who has heard all of the motivational speakers, read a lot of the self-development stuff out there and have been "talked to" for over two decades. The typical tactic of dangling a carrot in front of the donkey doesn't work with Zoomers anymore. What the Zoomer does respond to is an organic leadership approach that provides personalized motivation rather than one big rah-rah meant to fulfill everyone's needs.

The Zoomer employee is motivated by:

- ✓ Clearly outlined goals, processes and timelines.
- ✓ Leadership that provides the tools and leaves them alone.
- ✓ Paid sabbaticals to finalize a degree or take an extended trip.
- ✓ No restrictions on retirement or no mandatory retirement.
- ✓ The option to come back to work on contract if they retire.
- ✓ The opportunity to work in global offices.
- ✓ Leadership that deals with non-performers. Zoomers are demotivated quickly if they see that a slacker is getting away with not working.
- ✓ Leaders who provide tools and strategies to deal with ongoing change.

16: RECRUITING

As I write this we are still recovering from the recession. The US is still struggling with a high jobless rate. Canada is said to be in recovery with some job gains but just today in the *Vancouver Sun* I read that Air Canada was laying off over 1000 maintenance workers across Canada. So you might be wondering why we need to even spend time on recruiting. The truth is that finding good people is still at the top of the list for the best performing companies. In my research and in my conversations with executives they are telling me that finding good people remains a challenge.

Recruiting by generations is a little different than recruiting for a job. While we do not want to discriminate based on age it is prudent to look at what each generation brings to the table and see how that fits with job vacancies that your company may have.

Just like with regular recruiting you will want to know the following:

- ✓ What is the job description for the position!?
- ✓ What are the skills required to do the job?
- ✓ What skills are mandatory and which are negotiable or trainable?
- ✓ What is the time investment or hours a week needed for the job?
- ✓ What is the level of responsibility?
- ✓ What does "a day in the life" of the job look like?
- ✓ What are some known challenges of the job?
- ✓ What are the most attractive characteristics of the job?
- ✓ Who will the job applicant be interacting with?

A leader who does a good job of recruiting will take the time to go through these questions to ensure there is clarity at the outset and to increase the chances of finding the perfect fit. A lazy leader will simply say, "We need to hire someone," post an ad, do some interviews and make the hire.

If we are looking to make sure that the person we hire is a true fit we should also be asking the following questions of ourselves:

- ✓ Which generation is this job best suited to? For example, if the job is part time and task-oriented with little room for creativity, we may consider a late Zoomer (in their sixties)
- ✓ Which personality is best suited for this job?
- ✓ Who are the other people that will be interacting with this person and how will they get along with their generation and personality?

We also need to look at where the right people are going to look for jobs and we want to make sure we are there. For example, almost all of the generations go to web sites like monster.com but often a Gen Y will also check Craigslist, Twitter, Facebook or YouTube to find jobs. Creative employers should be posting their jobs in all of these forums. As an employer you want to be recruiting where your ideal employee will be. An HVAC company out of Portland figured out that their ideal employee was male, in his thirties, an avid outdoorsman who liked to do work that required physical labor. Based on that information they attended hunting and fishing trade shows and put up a booth—this has been their most successful recruiting method to date.

Savvy recruiting is going to be even more crucial in the future because companies do not have the luxury of hiring and training if the person they hired does not work out. Time invested in recruiting well is money earned in retention.

17: Retention

While companies have been downsizing and laying off employees in the past few years, the subject of retention is still of huge importance. Companies want to retain their best performers even in a down economy.

Some components of retention are applicable to all generations across the board. For example, everyone wants to work for a company that pays well. It used to be that money was not as important as compelling work but it turns out that money is a major motivating factor in deciding to stay with a company.

Each of the generations looks for certain things from an employer and I will share those, but first let me make it clear that retention no longer means a five or ten-year commitment with an organization. In today's work environment you would be lucky to keep a Gen Y for longer than two years. Because Gen X is looking for work–life balance you might see five years. Even Zoomers aren't looking for a ten-year job anymore—they are looking for project work or short-term work without committing to one employer for the long term.

You might think that this is bad news for employers, but in reality what it means is that employers have to get really good at the hiring, training and retention process. They need to ensure that they are adding time to the overall retention period but also that they have new talent available as replacements in shorter employment cycles.

As I have mentioned in previous chapters, Gen Y is looking for a friendly, open and fun environment. This is key to keeping Gen Y happy. Here are a few others:
- ✓ Ongoing training
- ✓ Latest technology

- ✓ School payment, tuition reimbursements
- ✓ Mentoring up (they mentor a Gen X or a Zoomer) opportunities
- ✓ Incentive trips/events/outings
- ✓ Interesting work aligned with their strengths
- ✓ Environmentally conscious companies
- ✓ Philanthropic companies
- ✓ Accessible leadership with little hierarchy.

Now for Gen X. Remember that Gen Xs are in their thirties, having families and looking to take the Zoomers' jobs. Keeping this in mind, here's what will keep a Gen X around longer:

- ✓ Career plans: when will they get promoted and make more money?
- ✓ Succession plans: who will they be replacing or what jobs will be created?
- ✓ Performance based pay
- ✓ Technology that makes their jobs easier
- ✓ Pay for their MBA or PhD
- ✓ Incentive trips for themselves and their families
- ✓ Family events that the company pays for
- ✓ Community outreach programs
- ✓ Recognition programs that include personalized rewards.

It used to be that we could count on Zoomers to take a job and stick around. We could almost always rely on them to be there. This is no longer true—more and more Zoomers see the merit in part-time work, project work or even going out on their own. So what keeps a Zoomer around?

- ✓ Compelling project focused work with definite outcomes
- ✓ Flexibility to choose how the work will get done
- ✓ Part-time and job-share options
- ✓ Technology that's easy to use and understand
- ✓ Contract work on a project-by-project basis
- ✓ Benefit programs that include options for elder care
- ✓ Work that allows them to lead teams
- ✓ Opportunities to train and teach.

A company I am consulting with right now has primarily Gen Y employees. When I told them that they must look at their talent in two-year cycles they asked me if this made them a "training" company. My response was that every company today is a training company, which quite simply means you invest in teaching and worry less about losing your investment. You are less likely to keep them around for any length of time if you don't invest in training anyway.

18: TRAINING

In the last chapter we talked about retention and I finished by saying that progressive companies need to be willing to invest in training all their people as well as adjusting the training to suit the learning style of each of the generations.

Companies have to morph their training and development programs into something far different from what worked for generations who grew up without the Internet.

Jeff is from a software company and leads a team of twenty-two employees spanning several generations. In an interview he said, "The (team members) who are right out of college are very different in their approach to learning and training. The Zoomer generation is comfortable with academic training in classrooms, whereas the new generation is more comfortable with on-demand learning and videos they can access when it is convenient for them."

Jeff added, "A new engineer goes online to find information when they have time, and the paper training manual is the last place they go for the answer to a technical question."

John, a senior vice-president of strategy, corporate development and emerging business for Nashua, NH-based SkillSoft, said that unlimited access to the Web has created a generation of multi-taskers with little patience and high expectations.

"This generation is used to writing term papers while listening to their iPods and browsing the Internet, which poses challenges with how to teach them," John said. "They have absorbed more information at their age level through their ears and eyes than any generation in mankind, and that impacts their learning preferences."

The Internet has made people impatient learners, so any company looking to engage and train Gen Y should take a multi-modal approach to training and have small chunks of content available 24–7, he said.

Gen Ys expect a lot from their employers. "Everything has happened so quickly for them and they are used to getting every bit of information they want in an instant. The negative there is that they are also more likely to move to another company, because information on other job opportunities is so readily available to them."

Gen Ys aren't as loyal to employers that don't allow them to grow. "I see with our clients that this generation is hard to retain because they are looking to make their mark—they learn skills quickly and want to move on, where older workers value their employer more and are a bit more loyal," John said.

The Zoomer generation may have read training manuals, but that doesn't work with Gen Y, or Gen X for that matter. If you hold training in a stuffy classroom they won't go. They want content in the form of podcasts or online courses. They expect compelling graphics. Mixing up learning modes is really appealing to this generation.

In order to provide training that appeals to Gen Y, X and Zoomers the following items need to be included:

- ✓ Multiple delivery mechanisms such as traditional books, online resources, interactive training, classroom training, courses through applications on smartphones, audio training and video training.
- ✓ Optional timelines for course completion such as "fast-track" options, evening learning options or weekend learning options as well as time provided while at work to complete learning.
- ✓ Learning materials made available on the Web.
- ✓ Mentoring and study buddies within the company to help support learning and keep each other on track.

The key is to adapt the training to the generation and offer a varied collection of classroom, online, and smartphone accessible learning.

19: Support

What does support look like in the workplace? No, we are not saying that we must become the emotional support center for our employees but we do need to look at support from a human needs perspective.

When I am working with clients I often say that we all need a certain level of psychology training to be the most effective we can be in the workplace. Daniel Goleman, the author of *Emotional Intelligence*, really broke ground by stating that EQ was more important than IQ. Leaders who have high EQs tend to enjoy higher morale in their groups and also tend to retain their employees for longer periods of time.

I mentioned empathy in Chapter Seven but support is different from empathy. When we support, we are looking at ways to help the other person to achieve success, whereas empathy is about putting yourself in the shoes of the other person and being able to communicate with that in mind.

Support needs will vary with the individual, but here is what each generation is looking for when it comes to support at work.

Some Zoomers would say that Gen Ys are needy because they are constantly looking for positive reinforcement. It always makes me chuckle when I see Gen Ys rebut a Zoomer on this topic. It's almost like Zoomers have internalized the school of hard knocks so the subconscious thinking is, "Suck it up, buttercup." Gen Y might argue that they have had hard knocks of their own but they are looking for support in their success.

Support for Gen Y is providing them with understanding when they are feeling emotional—have you noticed that Gen Ys are emotionally expressive? They are in touch with their feelings, so if they are having a bad day because they had a fight with their boyfriend or girlfriend they look to us to support them while still maintaining professional expectations. Recently my twenty-two-year-old daughter Courtney was very upset because her grandma had been ill ever since her grandfather had passed away. She was quite teary one day at work, and her boss was very supportive, saying, "Courtney, I am sorry to hear your grandma is sick. Do you need to leave early or is there anything you need from us?" This was the support that Courtney needed to feel good about her employer. She did not leave early but she was happy that the offer had been made. Really, it is about recognizing employees as humans and looking at how we can support them.

Support for a Gen X is a little different, but they are also looking for support that fits their stage in life. They are not looking for support just from their leaders, either—they are looking for team support. It is the leader's job to build an environment where everyone supports one another. Gen X is looking for "I've got your back" support to ensure their work is getting done while they are away. They are also looking for support concerning their family. That's why, if your company has built-in family activities or incentives, a Gen X is more likely to stick around and say engaged.

A Gen X is attracted to companies that have on-site daycare, daycare options and, as I mentioned earlier, the option to work flex hours. The challenge with flex hours that unless the department is set up to handle the work evenly it can be more stressful. This is why Gen X is looking for team support in getting work done and team support in getting the flextime.

Many Zoomers are faced with aging parents, teenagers at home and health challenges. Support for them is in the options provided by the company for situations like these. Many companies now give paid or unpaid leave for elder care and also offer counseling services.

Zoomers are reluctant to take time off to handle family or health issues because their work values say that you work no matter what your challenges are. Zoomers feel most supported when they are given a chance to take advantage of support programs and are not judged for their choice. A great example of this is how an employer handled a client of mine whose wife was diagnosed with leukemia. His company gave him the option of taking some time off but he chose to continue to work because it helped him cope. The company showed great support by insisting that he didn't have to work but honoring his decision without judgment.

20: PURPOSE

You might think that the word "purpose" does not relate to work but more and more people are looking at their jobs and asking themselves if their work is in alignment with their purpose.

Purpose is also a word used more for entrepreneurs than in corporate North America, but leaders who can link purpose to their teams' work can create higher levels of commitment and joy in those who work for them.

You can usually tell when someone is working within their personal purpose because they are generally joyful. Their work gets done easily and they feel they are contributing at a high level. Okay, you might be thinking, "Oh, please—how many people actually get to work within their purpose?" Leaders have an opportunity to link company purpose to an individual's skills and personal purpose. This is a coaching technique that can be pretty powerful so it is crucial to look at the natural inclinations of each generation.

Gen Ys are altruistic and idealistic—they constantly see people their age doing big things on reality TV so they believe that they too can make a big difference. They also have the sense that they can make a big impact if they are given the tools and the opportunities. A great way for leaders to link corporate and personal purpose for a Gen Y is to identify what values the company has in common with Gen Y and then provide ways Gen Ys can fulfill their own purposes while working for that company. A friend of mine has a daughter who would be considered a Millennial or a young Gen Y—she is in her teens. She created a business to sell jellybeans as "Ogopogo droppings" (Ogopogo is a fictional sea monster in Okanagan Lake in British Columbia). This young lady's goal is to sell enough of these to help kids in Africa; she has already helped a few families in Africa and I would say this young lady is definitely "on purpose." Another group, Free the Children, has a program called "Me to We," which is a group of Gen Ys all focused on the common goal of helping kids in underprivileged countries. I said earlier that Gen Y wants to work with philanthropic companies. If you can tie the work that a Gen Y does with something big like helping others they will definitely feel like they are working with their purpose.

Many Gen Xers are doing some pretty deep soul-searching at this stage in their lives. A recent article in *USA Today* stated that recent job losses and downsizing in corporate America has made Gen Xers re-think job stability—more specifically, creating their own stability. Gen X is the demographic that is starting businesses. They are looking at purpose and whether they want to continue to work just for the money, or work to create a balanced life with something more fulfilling.

I spoke at TEDxVancouver in the fall of 2009. The whole event was put together by a group of Gen Xers. Highly creative, highly engaged and highly effective, they put on a very successful TEDx event. When I spoke to the organizers after the event they said that the project was successful because all of them felt a part of something that was bigger than themselves. The TED brand is a global phenomenon (www.ted.com) so they knew that they had high standards to adhere to. The organizers also felt that they were on purpose because they were creating something that had never been attempted before in Vancouver. They were able to participate in something that, although it took hours away from their regular jobs, inspired and motivated them.

Leaders can link purpose to work by providing Gen X with projects that will make a big impact on the company and will gain them high profile with the executives and within the company on the successful completion of the project. I mentioned strengths earlier on in this book. When we look at purpose we need to also look at individual strengths and link the two together.

Purpose is a bit of a heavy topic for some Zoomers. At this stage in their lives and careers some are jaded and disillusioned. They scoff at the notion of working with a purpose because they still see work as work. They don't see the link between working to your purpose and creating joy at work.

Purpose is linked to happiness. When people feel they are using their talents to make a difference they are naturally more optimistic and joyful. Other Zoomers have made career choices based on purpose because they can no longer bear to do work that is "soulless." I am thinking of a client I am coaching right now as part of a team coach project I am doing with Teresia LaRocque. This client is currently working for her family's financial services business but she is desperate to leave and pursue what she really wants to do, which is buy and sell houses with her husband and do health coaching. She knows that her financial services job is not her purpose and she is willing to take the risk to do something she knows she will be happier doing. As leaders, we can guide Zoomers to what they would really like to be doing rather than going through the motions of work.

This can mean coaching someone to go to a different department or even to leave to pursue a long-held goal. We cannot underestimate the power of purpose in creating a happy workplace.

21: Life Balance

The title of an Internet article from September 2009 reads, "Bad Economy Hasn't Changed Gen Y's Desire for Work–Life Balance."

The article states that students still value work–life balance above all else when listing the top characteristics of an ideal entry-level employer, placing it well above other factors such as salary and meaningful work.

You might think that right now people are more concerned with getting a job in the first place and having job security. It would seem that work–life balance would be the last thing on their minds. Not for Gen Y, who has been pushing the envelope on what they want.

Remember that this is the generation that does not have the same security concerns we had at their age. Also remember that they are willing to live differently than we did at their age. Many of us left home and rented an apartment either by ourselves or with a roommate. Today a Gen Y has no problem with renting a house with eight roommates or staying at home to save money.

Work–life balance is also a high priority for Generation Xers. These latchkey kids felt the brunt of tripled divorce rates and hard working, dual-income parents. As a result, Gen Xers make different career choices to balance work and life. Many choose jobs closer to home over promotions. Others opt out of the workforce altogether to care for young children, or freelance.

What does this mean for employers relying on Gen X to take over from retiring Zoomers? It means looking at innovative ways to get the work done beyond the traditional methods practiced by the predominant Zoomer generation. As an illustration of work–life balance let's talk about how the generations decide what do to when sick with the flu.

The Zoomers have always been told that putting in the most and longest hours means you're a strong employee. Add in their competitive drive, and it can be downright impossible to feel comfortable taking a day off. A day away from the office means 80 million others could catch up, or worse—pass you up.

It's no wonder that Zoomers are not driven to stay home and heal; it's more a competition to see who can accrue the most unused sick days! The problem isn't whether or not companies have made it easier for Zoomers to take time off—it's that Zoomers still feel that it would be a sign of weakness. Surveys show that Zoomers will still go to work sick if they feel they have too much to do or if being sick would put them in the "wimp" category.

Compare that to Gen Xers, who vowed to never pay the same price for success as previous generations. Accruing sick days is not a badge of honor. Getting Xers to admit they're sick and need the time off is not a problem. The challenge with Xers is that their life stage makes every one of those sick days more valuable than any immunization.

Knowing when to cash in sick days or just go to work ill is the million-dollar question. Since they are not empty nesters, Xers know that when they are infected with the flu bug there is a good chance that the other birds in the nest will get sick, too. That means that regardless of how quick the Xer recuperates, it is likely they will need more time away to take care of the sick kids who can't go to school or to pitch in while their partner or spouse is down for the count.

What about Gen Y and sick days? For the 15 percent of Gen Ys who are still living with Mom and Dad, it can be a trip down memory lane, with homemade chicken noodle soup, plenty of TLC and reruns on TV. But even for those who have left the nest, sick days don't seem to be that big a deal.

The majority of Gen Ys don't have kids to worry about infecting and later caring for—and unlike Zoomers, they aren't worried that a day at home means they've gone off the grid. Gen Ys have never been defined by space and pace—so being at home and resting isn't that hard to embrace because they can still be online and feeling as much in the loop as ever.

22: Talent Pool

About four years ago I was speaking at an event in Kansas about the generations. I mentioned a concept from Europe that I predicted would become the norm within the next decade—a shared talent pool among organizations. I predicted that companies would hire with the intent to train, groom and guide their employees and once they have learned everything possible about the organization and there are no further learning opportunities they can then become part of a talent pool shared by like-minded organizations. These like-minded organizations might be in the same industry or in similar industries, but they would all hire with the intent to later share that person with their partner companies.

This concept holds great appeal for all of the generations because it opens the potential for learning and promotion. Imagine that you worked for Starbucks in their corporate office. You were given the best training and became very good at your job. At your regular coaching meeting with your boss you decide that there is really no other place you can go within the company to learn more or to expand your skills. Your evolved leader suggests that you enter the talent pool. You later get a call from McDonalds for a higher-level position than would have been available to you through Starbucks.

We all know that the best leaders are those who are willing to coach, groom and grow their people. We also know that all of the generations today are not easily wooed into sticking around if the work isn't challenging or if there are no signs toward growth in the future.

The talent pool idea is taking hold in Europe, with many companies recognizing that they would rather share their people within a group of "like" companies instead of losing the employee to another industry altogether.

Companies can form their own talent pools right away if they are already strategically aligned with other companies. Many great leaders informally set up a talent pool with their personal connections and keep these names and resources in their back pocket should one of their high performing employees want to move on.

Think of the hiring and recruiting attractiveness to any of the generations if you could offer them the endless opportunity of growth, learning and increased income potential through strategic alliances with other groups.

Some larger companies already have this in place. Companies such as Johnson & Johnson are already so massive, with hundreds of different departments as well as many global locations, that the need to create an outside talent pool may not be there. However, for mid-size companies it makes perfect sense to build strategic talent pools with other aligned organizations.

This is the future and I see this as being a major employment draw for all of the generations in the next few years.

23: Environment

I've already talked about environment at the beginning of the book when I discussed Zappos and how the employees decorate their areas to reflect each department's personality. That was just one example of the power of environment and how workplace shifts in layout can make each of the generations happier at work. In order to increase teamwork among the generations we need to look at the office environment and how it contributes to increased communication and teamwork.

Imagine that you walk into a workplace: all the offices are separated from each other and the main form of communication in the company is e-mail. Wait—am I describing your organization?

I have a current consulting client employing predominantly Gen Ys and the office is set up as one long hall with offices off the hall. It is no wonder that they are having communication challenges between departments—it is because the employees are all separated and do not make the effort to get up and talk to someone face to face. Of course face-to-face is not the constant form of communication we want to use but we do want to avoid heavy reliance on technology alone when communicating with our teams.

The atmosphere of a workplace is so important to how employees feel while they are there. Studies have shown that workplace environment has a direct impact on employee wellness and also happiness at work.

When Nintendo Canada moved from a two-story office in Richmond to a one-level office in Vancouver, the dynamics among the teams there shifted dramatically. Before with the two levels there was an "us versus them" feeling, but now that they are all on one floor they are quite literally all on the same level.

If your company occupies two floors there are things you can do to minimize the feeling of separation among work groups by having more frequent informal meetings, information updates and open dialogue about the challenges of a two-level or separated company environment.

You can also do what Zappos did by allowing each department to personalize their departments and add their own unique identifier that increases the bonds among teams and brings the company together.

I remember years ago coming up with creative ways to use environment to get better results with my teams but also to infuse humor. I found some tape that looked like police tape and would put it across my doorway when I didn't want to be interrupted. I also found a blue flashing light and when I was on the phone I would turn the light on so that everyone knew I was on the phone.

It is amazing how levity in the environment can increase employee happiness. Some thoughts for you are to ask how you could shift the current environment to be a happier workspace.

24: CHANGE

The workplace is changing and it is affecting the generations in different ways. As I mentioned earlier in this book, Zoomers do not plan to quit working at sixty-five, but the good news is that the Zoomers will be changing how they work. Zoomers do not want to work as long and hard as they have in the past. They are looking at changes in the workplace from an attitude of "do I want to be a part of these changes or am I ready to move?"

Zoomers are truly recognizing that change in the workplace is inevitable but they also want to be part of change if it results in more options. For example, a client I am coaching is a Zoomer in her early sixties. She has been working with a particular client for some time and now knows that there are some big changes that need to happen, but she just doesn't have the same drive or passion to do what is necessary to move forward. Her realization that she didn't have the energy for such a massive change led her to scale back her hours and outsource the big parts of the change project that she didn't want to tackle.

It is difficult to convince a Zoomer to change unless they can see the vision and the validation behind it. A lot of later-year Zoomers (in their sixties) are firmly in their comfort zones so resist change. Many companies have to train these Zoomers in change management or give them the options of moving on or staying to work through necessary change.

Change is good news for Gen Xers—they welcome it, they want it and they thrive on it. Unfortunately Gen X started their careers in a slow economy, made it through the rough economy of the early '90s and are now working in an economic climate that has been uncertain and unstable for everyone. Gen X is happy for change because they see it as an opportunity to finally move into senior management positions and also to spearhead change that the tired or uninterested Zoomer doesn't want to tackle. Gen X is well positioned to benefit in the next decade from the massive changes companies are implementing.

Gen Ys have lived in constant change all their lives and have become almost inured to it. The good news is that there is little resistance from the Gen Y with change; however, their lack of time on the job can make it a challenge for them to navigate change cycles that are perhaps familiar to the Zoomer or Gen X.

The key to managing all of the generations in change is that leaders must recognize psychological responses to change in addition to generational attitudes. The cycle of response to change is typically fear, resistance, anger, acceptance and finally transformation. Each generation has different perceptions of change, so it can incite a fight-or-flight response in a Zoomer, excitement and acceptance in a Gen X and perhaps apathy in the Gen Y, who is more than willing to go with the change but is looking for leadership to help get there.

Change conversations with each generation might include the following:

Zoomer: Your experience is needed to help us head in a new direction. It would be beneficial for you to include your Gen Xs and Gen Ys in the project to infuse with new viewpoints and ideas.

Gen X: We need you to spearhead this change as you have both the history and the technological knowledge to help us get there. We need you to bring in the Zoomer's back history and the Gen Y's creativity to move this forward.

Gen Y: We are going in this new direction. We need to you to provide your ideas while following the lead of Zoomers and Gen X, as they have the experience and knowledge of what has gone before.

25: Collaboration

Each generation has markedly different styles and preferences in how they communicate and work together. How can we create an environment where these disparate tribes can come together?

Let's look again at Gen Y's preferences at work:

- ✓ Constant access to the Internet
- ✓ Use desktop collaboration tools without a second thought
- ✓ Expect to always be connected
- ✓ E-mail isn't an important tool for them; social networking is
- ✓ Phones are preferred devices, although not necessarily for the voice applications.

Gen Ys are organized around their interests, establishing very casual connections via social networking with people they may have never met.

Gen X's work preferences are:

- ✓ Internet-centric, but just starting to think about life without a landline phone
- ✓ Socially organized around school and work associations
- ✓ Not naturally collaborative
- ✓ Cynical and skeptical, but enamored with technology.

At work, Zoomers are:

- ✓ Connected by desktop or laptops, and less web-focused
- ✓ Restrictive about norms and business processes
- ✓ Experienced enough in the workplace to know what works for them
- ✓ Originally non-conformists, but expect people to conform
- ✓ Fans of standardization.

Their comfort level with technology varies widely. They're not technology adverse, but they've developed styles and preferences that are not likely to change.

One generation's way of working doesn't always mesh well with another's. The others view what is normal to Gen Y—pulling out a laptop at a meeting or checking e-mail during a presentation—as disrespectful. Gen Ys are not great with having to work in structured timeframes and they don't work well with schedules. Gen Xers and Zoomers prefer to work in real time; Gen Ys are comfortable in non-real time, collaborating via blogs or Facebook.

The question then is, what can leaders do to help such different generations work together? How do you build an environment conducive to collaboration?

There's a technology angle. How do you pick products and services for collaboration that don't force users into a style that's not comfortable for them?

You have to give people the freedom to work in the way that brings out their productivity. They're not going to change their style. Forcing someone who prefers a mobile device into a desktop-bound environment, or vice-versa, isn't good for them or the enterprise.

People always default to the easiest-use alternative. Leaders should look for flexible devices and solutions that lend themselves to customization. Make the tools suit the users, not the other way around.

Part of a leader's role is understanding the company's corporate culture. What things are flexible and what are not? At Cisco, meetings don't always start on time but a rigid adherence to schedule is less important than allowing people to say what they think. A leader needs to analyze what the corporate culture's values are and find tools to enable those priorities.

Leaders should put together a checklist for collaborative tools. What are the requirements—the mandatory features, followed by the nice-to-haves? I suggest that leaders purposely survey their team members along generational lines. What are the requirements cited by Zoomers? By Gen Ys? It's the leader's job to find the common ground.

26: TECHNOLOGY

Is it rude if Gen Ys use their BlackBerrys in a meeting? If they are using Twitter or other social media then it can actually be a good thing for you and your business. Recently I spoke at an HR conference and they had a Gen Y on-site Tweeter—she tweeted every few minutes about what was going on with the conference. Rude? Nope. Just keeping non-conference attendees up to date with minute by minute information.

Recently, business information solutions provider LexisNexis released the results of a study that examined how technology was used in the American workplace. The study's focus was on differing opinions among generational groups. The findings? The generation gap at work features vast discrepancies when it comes to each generation's opinion of the appropriate use of technology—a problem that leads to tension in the workplace.

The survey compared technology and software usage among generations of working professionals, including Zoomers (ages 44–60), Generation X (ages 29–43) and Generation Y (age 28 and younger). The total sample size was 700 legal and white-collar professionals with 250 coming from the legal profession.

According to the survey:

✓ Two-thirds of Zoomers agree that Personal Digital Assistants (PDAs) like the BlackBerry and cell phones contribute to a decline in proper workplace etiquette, and believe the use of a laptop during in-person meetings is "distracting." Less than half of Gen Ys agree.

✓ Just 17 percent of Zoomers believe using laptops or PDAs during in-person meetings is "efficient," while more than one-third of Gen Ys do.

✓ Only 28 percent of Zoomers think blogging about work-related issues is acceptable, while 40 percent of Gen Y workers do.

Yikes! Phones and PDAs are distracting and inefficient tools? Blogging is unacceptable? Who are these people? Unfortunately, they're the people who still have a lot of power when it comes to the decisions made at the workplace. Zoomers are the executives, the CEOs, the bosses, while Gen Y is just now getting a foot in the door. But it's clear that these two generations strongly disagree on how technology is to be used.

This disagreement often shows up most clearly in meetings, with laptop-created versus handwritten notes or minutes. Zoomers and Gen X still like handwritten, whereas Gen Y sees note taking as what they do on their PDAs.

Another issue being faced is the blurring of boundaries between work and home. Gen Y workers generally don't see a problem accessing personal web sites like Facebook and blogs from work. In fact, 62 percent of Gen Y professionals access a social network on the job, but only 14 percent of Zoomers do. That discrepancy could have something to do with the fact that Gen Y spends a lot more of their day online—they spend 10.6 hours per day accessing social networks, news sites, blogs, forums, and multimedia sharing sites, versus only 5.6 hours reported by Zoomers.

The study also found that Gen Y workers multi-task at higher levels, but it's here that the numbers get kind of confusing. According to the report, Gen Y workers spend an average of 22.9 hours per day using e-mail, web browsers, instant messaging (IM) and productivity applications, while Zoomers reported 10.3 hours with the same programs. But seriously, 22.9 hours? That begs the question: when does Gen Y eat or sleep? Who even stays up for 22.9 straight hours? The problem apparently comes from how the question was asked. Respondents were asked to report on how much time they spent on each of four types of applications in an average workday. The average time reported for "using" each application every day added up to a total of 15.9 hours, much longer than the standard eight-hour work day.

What this actually means is that workers are keeping many applications open at the same time and accessing them concurrently. While the data could have been presented in a more straightforward manner, the end result is that Gen Y switches back and forth between applications far more than the Zoomers do.

In reality, the future requires merging ideals in regards to using and accepting technology.

27: RECOGNITION

In tough economic times, employers are often asked to do more with less. When recognition and incentives are cut along with workers, hours and perks, productivity and employee engagement suffer.

Building a culture of recognition can reverse a downward employee engagement spiral. Business futurists Roger Herman and Joyce Gioia report that statistics show companies that recognize their people outperform companies that don't by 30 to 40 percent. In addition to driving business results, recognition and incentives change employee culture—encouraging loyalty, engagement and enthusiasm for the job. Recognition is a form of feedback especially valued by Gen X and Y employees.

A culture of recognition exists in organizations that catch people doing the right things right. In these organizations:

✓ Recognition is a corporate value, operating at every level.
✓ Recognition happens informally and formally. Improvement is rewarded, not just top performers.
✓ Reward programs are customized. Employees choose rewards meaningful to them—another hot button with Gen X and Y.
✓ Best practices—behaviors and activities that get results—are identified, cloned and rewarded.

The influx of Gen X and Y into the workforce has increased the importance of a culture of recognition. These generations were raised on feedback, recognition and reward. They thrive in a supportive environment that values their unique contributions and rewards them, not just as a collective group, but in personal, individual ways as well.

In a culture of recognition, just any recognition won't do. The most effective recognition rewards the right behaviors immediately. Recognize your people for behaviors and activities based on best practices—well defined, credible standards that align with and support corporate goals. Simply put, best practices are those behaviors and activities exhibited by your top performers. The goal is to turn best practices into common practices. To determine your best practices, engage management to:

- ✓ Identify your top performers. Everyone knows who they are—the ones who are good collaborators and get the job done. They close the most sales, get commitments that put checks in the bank and quickly fix problems and move on to the next opportunity.
- ✓ Find out how those top performers do what they do. Ask these five basic questions: How's it going? What's contributing to your success? What are your obstacles? If you had a magic wand and could add, change or delete anything today, what would it be? How are you recognized for doing what management wants you to do?
- ✓ Define what you need in terms of behaviors and results. Based on the answers to these questions, identify two or three behaviors your top performers use to get the results you're looking for. Choose two behaviors (quality/quantity) and one result metric (productivity indicator). In sales, for example, do not reward people simply for sales made. Instead reward them for targeting ten key clients and going after the knowledge they need (behaviors). Then reward them for closing the targeted sales (results).
- ✓ Reward people on the spot for achieving these behaviors. It's not always easy. Managers must be on the ball to observe, evaluate and reinforce new behaviors. That's coaching!

Zoomers find hard work a reward in itself but Gen X and Y demand feedback and thrive on recognition. As the most-coached generations, they want to know how they are doing and how they can be more successful faster. They expect timely rewards or the reward's effectiveness is diminished. They want public recognition in front of peers. Recognition says to them, "I've noticed you. I want you to be successful." Make recognition and rewards timely and public, and your Gen X and Y employees will reward you with continuous performance improvement.

28: Gossip

Zoomers will remember the water cooler or the lunchroom gossip. When I think of gossip I think of an episode on *The Office* where Michael the branch manager spreads gossip about every employee because he wants to appear as if he is in the know and hip with what is happening with everyone.

Let's face it—everyone loves gossip. In fact, Gen Y has grown up with instant access to pop culture and excessive gossip with bloggers like Perez Hilton or the celebrity gossip site and TV show *TMZ*.

Since gossip in the workplace is unavoidable, some companies are actually encouraging gossip using technology. Best Buy America has an online forum where team members can "gather around the water cooler" online. They also have a forum for sharing positive gossip, like staff getting married or having babies. It is not a forum for negative gossip and interestingly, by sharing positive gossip across all generations, it leads to increased morale and team camaraderie.

One definition of gossip is "a form of communications that an individual participates in for the purpose of discussion, or passing onto to others; hearsay information."

Gossip is being extended to the individuals outside the company as well as the Internet allows the public to openly "gossip" about their employers.

Office gossip sites might be the next wave in sites for job seekers to review. Some of these sites are glassdoor.com, JobVent.com and vault.com. Many employees are visiting the sites and writing about the companies that they work for or have worked for. These sites allow employees to confidentially and/or anonymously post information about company interview processes, company culture, specific management styles, benefits, salaries, bonuses, workspace and anything else you can think of to comment about. Comments range from "great company with strong benefits" to "avoid manager of highway design based in corporate office, as he micromanages."

Should companies be concerned? Yes. Should employees take the time to comment on their company's culture, management style, benefits, salaries, etc.? Sure. Should job seekers review these sites? Yes, with caution. These sites have now evolved to include happy, satisfied employees' reviews of their employers as well as direct, not-so-positive critiques. Companies need to regularly monitor these sites and make sure that information posted is relevant and not just a disgruntled employee looking to slam the company. Companies can use the information as informal employee surveys—a way to take a pulse from an anonymous group. That being said, anonymous reviews should be read with a critical eye. I'll address this again under the value of these sites to job seekers.

Should employees take the time to comment on companies?

Yes, if you, as an employee, can write an honest evaluation of your current or past employer then you should. Discuss the interview process, company culture, benefits, bonuses, etc. Is your workspace comfortable? Does the company encourage and pay for additional training? Does it encourage involvement in professional associations? What did you want to know about a company before you joined it? Try to be constructive, but honest, in your critique.

Do you recall the children's game called "Pass It On"? Rarely does the comment at the start of the game end up as the same comment at the end of the game. Remember, not only are there at least two sides to every story, those stories over time aren't always remembered accurately.

29: Office Politics

Just like office gossip, we always have office politics and likely always will as long as people work together. Office politics can be highly destructive and can backfire on the person who plays games.

Some examples of office politics are speaking behind someone's back, saying one thing to someone's face and something else to others, undermining a peer or colleague to make them look bad, procrastinating on a team project due to personality conflicts and many others.

A client of mine naively thought that by letting one employee know that they were watching the performance of her peer they were simply keeping the employee in the loop. In reality what happened is that the employee who was told her peer was on "watch" began to hope and believe that she could have her peer's job. This was not the truth—the owners were giving the peer a chance to improve performance. This seemingly innocent communication created a classic scenario for office politics. Leaders have to be cautious of what they promise and how they communicate to avoid adding to the office's political environment.

Generational issues such as those we've already covered can create office politics. For example, take the Zoomer who refuses to retire. This forces other employees to stay in one position too long when they would normally move up. Sometimes an entry-level new hire ends up in the same position as an employee who has been with the company for more than ten years. Such a situation creates friction between employees, not because they have a personal problem with each other, but because of the generation gap. If you are the fresh graduate who has just found a job, you should expect this to be one of the challenges that you will be facing—fast.

When work ethics come into play, different opinions on how to get things done could be easily magnified into office politics. The Zoomer generation may use the same techniques that have been proven effective over a long time while the Gen Y innovates and looks for ways on how to make things better. That might become a source of conflict as everyone will insist the team follow their procedure.

This is where give and take comes in. It is actually not a matter of generations anymore but rather how to make things better by injecting a few ideas from younger workers. Successful fusion of ideas is not guaranteed but the mere fact that everyone is contributing to develop a better way to deal with things is already a step forward.

But what if there is a need to have only one idea? This would usually happen when you are in a meeting and everyone has to present something. It is inevitable that ideas clash among generations.

Think about it: even in one generation we might not agree with one another's ideas so it's just common sense that our ideas will bump against each other with those of a person from a different generation.

At this point, everyone loses if they insist that their idea is better. Managers and supervisors should be smart enough to act as go-betweens and make a decision everyone can live with. The manager may have some biases but they are in a better position to judge the merit of each idea since he or she will hear all sides of the story.

Office politics are often cured by open communication and increased training on generational and personality differences. Leaders need to create an environment that fosters dialogue, not backbiting or office politics.

30: Unique Abilities

Unique abilities can be viewed as similar to strengths and purpose but here we are looking at individuals and how their unique abilities help move team efforts forward. Let's look at unique abilities as more of a gift than a strength. Individuals can have unique abilities that are linked to their generation. For example, a Zoomer could have a unique ability to be a wonderful leader due to their on-the-job experience over time.

A good leader is a good coach. They focus on helping those they lead to be the best they can be, and provide them with training and incentives to continue to grow and develop. A fantastic leader will recognize the unique abilities of their individual staff members and will even guide them to pursue dreams in alignment with their unique talents, even if it means going somewhere else.

I had a boss who made an indelible impact on me in this regard way back when I was in finance. I had been in the banking industry and then the insurance industry and from there went to work for a credit union. My boss, Linda, was incredibly supportive and intuitive. We had many conversations about my dreams, goals and unique abilities. When I confessed to her that I wanted to be self-employed as a consultant and author she actually supported me toward that goal instead of trying to keep me working for her. I was bringing in lots of revenue for her branch as the mortgage development manager and by letting me pursue my dreams she would have to replace me. Her parting words to me were to follow my heart, and that she believed I would be highly successful because of my unique abilities.

As leaders we can steer people to follow the path that makes them the most happy. A lot of leaders try to placate people or promise them things that they know may never come true and I think this is a dishonest form of leadership.

Strong leaders with healthy self-esteem are not jealous of the unique abilities of their staff. Instead they see the greatness in others and they do all they can to support that greatness—even if it means a promotion above them or moving on to something else.

A Zoomer boss I coached had a Gen Y who was extremely fast at picking up the technology of the department and within three months she was coming up with ideas and solutions that would increase productivity for the company. The Zoomer boss was noticing her own feelings of jealousy and she mentioned this to me in our coaching session. First of all, I congratulated her for her honesty. Then we talked about how she could nourish the unique abilities of her Gen Y instead of holding her back. The Zoomer boss went back and created a new position for the Gen Y and two things happened: the Gen Y continued to make the department more productive and she became unfailingly loyal to her Zoomer boss and refused an offer from a competing company.

In the bigger picture of individual goals, dreams and unique abilities we do not hoard talented people for our own selfish ends, we help them grow and get to where they want to go. This always pays back in spades as we will attract other talented people, and the people that we have helped groom and grow will always return the great favor by referring people to us or even referring us to other opportunities.

The concept of unique ability is really about honoring the difference in each of us—treating people with respect and honoring their abilities. Leaders who focus on building people up are never at a loss when it comes to attracting highly talented and gifted people.

31: Time Off

I mentioned in earlier sections that each of the generations view work uniquely. We know that Zoomers have an innate work ethic that we often jokingly refer to as "work, work, work and then you die." Gen X is looking for balance with family time and Gen Y's motto is "life is first and work is second." New generations of leaders often have a completely different way of working than their older counterparts. They also view time off as a more valuable commodity than a raise or a promotion. One Gen Y who now works for a client of mine demanded three weeks' vacation rather than the standard two. They gave it to her because they knew it was a deal breaker for her.

While the Zoomer generation usually views long hours as evidence of loyalty and hard work, Gen X and Y tend to try to have more work–life balance. They've seen their parents' limited quality of life and the lack of loyalty that companies showed to their hard-working parents in the 1990s, and they're not impressed. They want flexible hours, more vacation time, continuous training and telecommuting options. They expect to leverage technology to work efficiently instead of staying late in the office to get it all done.

Zoomers have traditionally felt that you have to pay your dues to your company—and if you hate your job, that's just part of life. They also believe that you have to work longer to earn longer vacations. Generations X and Y typically don't accept this; they want rewarding, intellectually stimulating work—and they don't want someone watching them too closely to check on their progress. They also want more vacation time as part of their conditions of hire. These new groups are independent, creative and forward thinking. They celebrate cultural diversity, technology and feedback, and they prefer more of a "lattice" or individualized approach to management as opposed to the traditional "corporate ladder."

Several Fortune 500 companies are changing their entire organizations to meet the wants and values of the newer generations. Here are some examples:

A large US accounting firm gives four weeks of vacation to every new hire (most US companies offer only two weeks). This firm also offers new parents classes on how to reduce their working hours to spend more time with their families.

A software company in Silicon Valley has no set office hours. Staff come in and work when they choose. Everyone gets paid time off every month to do volunteer work, and they get a six-week sabbatical every four years.

If you think these dramatic policies would never work and would be too costly, then remember—these are all very profitable, highly productive companies with low staff turnover. They've made new rules, and they're successful.

As a result, if you're a member of a team whose leadership is being passed from an older generation leader to a new generation leader, you'll probably need to adjust to having more autonomy, more high-level tasks delegated to you, and to finding that the boss may not be around as much to check on things.

The new generations value action, so they'll work more efficiently and productively to earn time off. They'll expect their team to work hard too, but they'll also know when it's time to leave the office and go play. One of the ways in which they gain this efficiency is by using technology.

32: PERFORMANCE

After just a few weeks working for one firm, Generation Y employees can become bored and may look to leave if their performance is not managed effectively. They crave constant feedback and close contact with their managers. Zoomers have become accustomed to an annual performance review process and Generation X has had to endure 360-degree performance reviews. In this chapter we look at performance from generational perspectives.

A large project involving unknown technology and a short timeline might be approached differently by each of the generations. If we were to rate performance by "did the job get done," which of these scenarios would appear to you to indicate high performance?

Gen Y quickly IMs all of their peers to ask if they have heard of the technology and posts a tweet asking the same question. They do some quick research on their PDA. Then they gather a group of people and share what they know about the technology so far. They get the team working on the project segments as a group, with group reporting.

Gen X checks in with the Zoomer lead who delegated the project to ask a few clarifying questions, asks for resources and does some research on the Web on their laptop. If Gen X can't find what they need on the technology they call a group meeting and delegate one or two team players to source it, while systematically planning how to meet the timelines of the project.

The Zoomer looks at the resource manual sent with the technology, calls the technology developer and talks to key people to find out what they need to know about the technology to take the project forward. Zoomer takes it upon himself or herself to compile all that they've learned about the technology, presents it to the working group and also presents the project timeline he or she completed on their own. They ask for team buy-in to achieve the timeline.

If you chose just one of these scenarios as indicating high performance you would be incorrect. The correct answer is "all of the above." Each generation uses the resources they are most comfortable with and end up at the same place, albeit in very different ways. As we judge performance we need to look at end results, not the way we got there. Of course, if in your industry it's life or death if a process isn't followed in a precise way then that process would win over a creative approach. However, most industries can allow flexibility in how teams get to the end result and still rate them as high in performance.

33: TENURE

Union groups are struggling with the pressure that Gen Ys are placing on the concept of tenure in the workplace. Gen Y is not too keen on being told that they cannot get vacation, promotions or recognition unless they stick around for a long period of time. They also do not give instant respect to someone who has been on the job a long time. It's especially true if that person is completely incompetent but the comment the Gen Y hears when they make an observation about it is, "Oh, she has been here forever—she has always been that way."

Zoomers, on the other hand, started out in post-industrial workplaces that really ingrained in them a belief that staying loyal to your employer would be rewarded. The Zoomer loyal-to-the-employer mindset is in contrast to the Gen Y's and has created the impression among Zoomers that Gen Ys are not loyal. In fact, it's just that we are comparing two distinctly different experiences. Zoomers tried to be loyal but many were downsized and had to find new jobs. The Gen Y children witnessed this. Based on this Gen Y developed an aversion to being loyal to an employer. Instead they are loyal to themselves and their happiness.

Gen X views tenure from a frustrated point of view because they have done the time with the promise of promotion and raises, only to be told that the Zoomers were not going anywhere for another ten years.

If we look at organizations as performance-based cultures we can see that an organization that rewards tenure over performance is going to have morale and productivity challenges. Studies have shown that companies focused on performance rather than tenure exhibit greater creativity, greater results and happier clients. A performance-based culture typically has higher levels of customer satisfaction than a tenure-focused one. Of course, if all your company has is high performing employees of long tenure then you are in an enviable position (at least until they retire) but in my experience some level of turnover is healthy for an organization and for the people in that organization.

I remember when I worked in banking my boss was a true Traditionalist (parents of the Zoomers). I had joined the bank right after high school and got promoted each of the ten years that I was with the bank. In my tenth year I was headhunted away by an insurance company and when I told my boss he was horrified. His Traditionalist attitude was that I had to stick it out with the company to have a successful career. He told me I would lose my pension and that once I left I could never come back. As a Gen X I was more motivated to work for a smaller, private company where I could make a bigger impact, plus I was offered $10,000 more per year in salary. I made the choice to leave and since the new company was focused on performance the fact that I was new to them had no bearing on the value they believed I could bring to their organization.

Organizations need to re-think tenure and how they reward it. If we are just rewarding time on the job we could be sending the wrong message—a message that will completely demotivate the Gen Xs and Gen Ys we are striving to keep around for a while.

34: Union Workplaces

As I mentioned in the previous chapter, tenure is a difficult concept for Gen Y to grasp. This will be a fundamental challenge for unions in the future.

In the past the union movement's core supporters have been Zoomers who work full-time, continuous workers committed to an industry, or even a company. Few new workers or Gen Ys will fit this mould. If Generation Y's life patterns pan out as predicted, it will be a decade or more before many of them commit to the obligations that keep people in work whether they like it or not—namely a mortgage and children. Zoomers have looked for the job security of a union environment whereas Gen Y is looking at money and education.

For many, especially those who are well educated and confident, job insecurity doesn't concern them greatly. If they're unhappy with management or conditions, most won't choose to join a union, mobilize other workers and fight for better conditions. They will turn on their heels and leave, maybe grumbling a little in their exit interview (if, in fact, they even do one). After all, who takes out insurance on a shared house they're just renting?

But this isn't the end of the story. Generation Y's men and women take the work–life balance seriously. Generation Yers talk about working smarter, not harder. They talk about working from home, moving away from the daily nine-to-five grind and working to live rather than the other way around. They don't want to be absent, work-obsessed fathers or harried working mothers. They don't want to be company slaves. This goes against the traditional work model that most Zoomers have adhered to which is "work is a place you go and you stay until the job is done."

Gen Ys are also a generation deeply skeptical about the ethics of corporations so they don't pledge loyalty to an employer automatically. This is a natural reaction for a generation born in the 1980s, the first era of downsizing, deregulation and leaner, meaner corporations.

Generation Yers saw their Zoomer parents dismissed from their jobs (even in union environments) after years of service, all for the sake of a profit margin. They have also seen their parents' physical and emotional lives suffer as a result of overwork.

This skepticism extends to other institutions and explains another barrier unions face. Gen Yers have been bombarded with advertising all their lives and have learned to filter it out. To these people, propaganda and class-consciousness are both just so much white noise.

The unions that Gen Ys are joining—and even with 13 percent membership, unions still have more Gen Y than other comparable organizations—are those that have recognized the problem and offer something tangible. A range of unions representing teachers and nurses, electricians and builders, and actors and journalists is recruiting members straight out of the education system, often with innovative programs such as a year's free or cheap membership to introduce young people to the notion of collective representation. When unions market themselves on the basis of the services they provide, the pitch invariably works.

Unions are also changing the way they campaign by using savvy and engaging takes on issues of broad community concern such as the war in Iraq, refugees and tying that into the attack on workers' rights. Their current TV ads and on-the-ground campaigns around rights at work have shown mass action doesn't have to be about angry workers breaking down the barricades.

The biggest opportunity for unions is to tackle the "bad" employees who have let the union protect them instead of dealing with poor performance. Gen Y will definitely not stick around if they see double standards.

The Zoomers and Gen X in the union environment have a very challenging job ahead of them. The realities of Gen Y's work mindset are coming up hard and fast against the rigid rules and hierarchy that have held unions in good stead up until this point.

The future success of unions is going to rely on their willingness to transform the traditions and modernize their approach to meet the current realities of today's workforce.

35: Middle Management

I predict that middle management as it is structured in most companies now will soon be a thing of the past. I am seeing evidence of this happening in companies I am currently working with. As Gen Y moves up the ranks they are less enamored with being solely in charge and are much more interested in lateral power sharing. They would much rather share a project or a responsibility with others.

This might trouble a Zoomer because Zoomers are from the corporate world of "each man or women for himself or herself," aiming forever to be the one at the top. Gen X has been tirelessly pursuing the executive level and has come up against the "gray ceiling" of the Zoomers who are staying put.

If we look at the organizational charts of most large corporations middle management levels are prevalent. Some would argue they are necessary to keep the company efficient. But if we look at the effect that Gen Y is having on traditional business models we would see that Gen Y is perfectly comfortable relating to the executive level, and actually prefers it. They expect to work in an environment where they can talk to anyone and not have to adhere to hierarchy.

Demographically it is mostly Zoomers and Gen X who currently hold middle-management positions and not everyone is happy.

The Gen X middle manager is actually quite frustrated at working long hours with no immediate sign they'll get beyond their current title. Some organizations counter this by changing the title while leaving the job essentially the same—these are old fashioned ploys to basically "shut them up" for a bit. Throughout this book I have talked about what all of the generations want at work and the most important thing we all want is interesting work where we can feel a sense of accomplishment and contribution.

The middle manager often feels powerless and stuck due to corporate structure. I see a future where middle management is changed into leaders who manage projects, working with other project leaders on a team. These projects contribute to company growth and solving "people working together" challenges. In this structure a project leader isn't on his or her own; rather, they have other team leads to refer to. This structure allows for vacations, flex work schedules, part time and working from home—all of the perks that Gen X is looking for.

Gen Y is not attracted to middle-management jobs, which appear to be a lot of hard work for very little return. They would much rather do team jobs with technology and not have to do the same amount of work as their Gen X predecessors. My daughter Courtney is twenty-two. She is going to college while working part time, but has been offered management positions. Each time she is asked she has declined. When asked why, she says, "It seems to be a huge amount of responsibility without too much extra compensation. I would just rather keep doing my job with the flexibility and freedom it gives me." Spoken like a true Gen Y.

36: SENIOR MANAGEMENT

So if the future workplace will not have middle managers and instead will have job teams with multiple leaders, what does that mean for senior management roles?

In a survey conducted by PDI of 24000 senior managers in Minneapolis, both Zoomers and Gen X are able to meet performance outcomes, although they arrive there very differently.

Zoomers were 18 percent more likely to be rated as "knowing the business" and 10 percent more likely to use technical or functional expertise on the job. They also rated better in their ability to coach and develop people and manage project execution.

Generation X managers received higher ratings in self-improvement, work commitment, and analyzing issues.

Women's senior management styles and personality traits in the traditional workplace mirror many of the values that Generation Xers bring to senior management positions. Women are by nature more collaborative, partnership-oriented, consultative, adaptive and conciliatory than men. These feminine traits will become increasingly valued over the next decade.

Where Zoomers in senior management have remained somewhat aloof and removed from the front line, Gen X has gotten a little closer because they have Gen Ys reporting to them and they recognize Gen Y's need for familial relationships with their co-workers.

Zoomers in senior management tend to have the following behaviors:
✓ A little unreachable or give the impression that they are
✓ Close the door when having discussions and only include the stakeholders

- ✓ An attitude of "the buck stops here": little room for negotiating a major decision
- ✓ A sense of entitlement to all the perks from clients, and reluctant to pass those perks along.

A Gen X in senior management tends to have the following behaviors:

- ✓ Approachable, friendly and even collegial
- ✓ Closes the door rarely and even then would prefer to maybe take the person for a walk or a coffee so that it isn't an "across the desk'" scenario
- ✓ An attitude of "Let's get creative here, before we make a final decision."
- ✓ Willingness to share the perks from clients with others on the team.

Recently I worked with a major games company in Canada. The CEO is a Gen X who has been with the company for quite some time. His team consists of primarily Gen Xs as well. I was struck by how accessible he was to his team during my session on developing the strengths of the generations. There we were in the boardroom, revealing each person's strengths as well as their areas for development and Ron was very comfortable interacting on the same level as his management team.

I know for a fact that had he been a Zoomer he would have struggled a little more with such a level of transparency. Because Ron showed up as open, uncensored and willing to learn, his entire team participated at the highest level possible and we created fantastic results.

37: COMMUNICATION

In my first book *Say What You Mean, Mean What You Say* I provide solutions on how to communicate. The book covers the foundations of effective communication such as assertive language, move-forward language and the importance of understanding communication styles for different personality types.

That book was written in 2001 but the elements of good communication are still true today. An added communication challenge we have now is understanding how to communicate with the generations to get the best results.

Understanding how to communicate with a Driver, Dancer, Detailer or Deflector helps us get better results with other people. The same holds true for the generations. Each generation has its own buzzwords: personalized language and words that motivate.

Let's look at the Gen Ys first and see how we can best communicate with them. Gen Ys use instant messaging on Facebook or direct messaging on their smartphones constantly. They are used to acronyms and shortened versions of regular words. They also use endearments or nicknames for their friends. My daughter Courtney, who is twenty-two, calls almost all of her friends by their last names, not their first names, as do most of her friends.

In the workplace it would depend on the level of familiarity and also the industry but generally Gen Ys like a work environment where they are free to use nicknames and informal language. Here are some tips on building great rapport with a Gen Y:

✓ Use short words and even instant messaging style if communicating with them via smartphone

- ✓ Gen Ys feel that e-mail is archaic and would much rather send you a document via MSN, Facebook or Skype. However, they will use e-mail, preferring the content to be short, sweet and to the point.
- ✓ If your work environment is open and flexible, encourage nicknames for the team. They really enjoy this type of connection.
- ✓ Get up to speed on Twitter, YouTube and other social media. This is how they get their news.
- ✓ Keep your tone and approach highly positive. Gen Y responds to a positive approach and does not receive criticism the same way Gen X and Zoomers do. Use an approach that says, "Here is what you do well and here is where you need help, so here are your options to learn to do better."
- ✓ Gen Ys do not respond to bullying tactics or "do this or you're fired" approaches. They would much rather quit than put up with an autocratic work environment, believing life is too short.

Generation Xers are fairly easy to communicate with because they have learned to bridge the communication styles of both the Zoomers and the Gen Ys. Savvy Gen Xers have become accustomed to the Zoomers' hard work mentality and have learned to adapt their communication style to meet the needs of their Zoomer bosses and counterparts. Gen X also has the advantage of technological knowledge to help them relate to Gen Ys.

I actually consider many Gen Xs control freaks—my book *The Control Freak Revolution* was aimed at this demographic. The best ways to communicate with Gen X are:

- ✓ Gen Xs are striving for promotions and to take over from the Zoomers, so using language that recognizes their contributions will go a long way.
- ✓ Control freaks with their time, Gen Xs are all about efficiency, time management and project timelines. Make sure you respect this and adhere to their need for these things when approaching them.
- ✓ Gen X can be impatient with the Zoomer who complains, because they feel that somebody just needs to "do it."

- ✓ Use language that gets to the point and provides resources right away. Gen X does not feel that it can take the time to beat around the bush.
- ✓ Gen Xs are now having families so they are trying to squeeze as much work into their work hours as possible. Resist asking them to put in weekend time or evening time as this generation wants to balance work with family life.
- ✓ Provide real career potential for Gen X.

Communicating with Zoomers is fairly easy for other Zoomers, but can be frustrating for Gen Ys and sometimes Gen Xs. Remember, Zoomers have a "work hard and then die" mentality so their expectations and the way they communicate can seem to be focused on "all work and no fun."

The best ways to communicate with a Zoomer are:
- ✓ Provide evidence that something will get done by showing a deadline or project update.
- ✓ Speak in a more professional manner and respect their position.
- ✓ When sending e-mail include clear expectations and do not blind copy everyone and anyone.
- ✓ Respect lines of authority in the workplace by not going behind your boss's back to their boss. Communicate directly to your boss or peers.
- ✓ Do not blindside a Zoomer by withholding information they need for their boss or for an important meeting.
- ✓ Keep it direct, professional and to the point while staying friendly. Don't go on about your boyfriend or girlfriend troubles.
- ✓ Use assertive language that is solution based, such as "I will do this" or "We could expand our business by… " Don't say, "The way we do this sucks."

Communication will always be an ongoing challenge in the workplace and understanding the best ways to approach the generations can help us all get along better and get better results.

38: CULTURE

Another factor in understanding the whole person is their cultural background. This includes heritage but also their environment while growing up. Culture and childhood environment are factors that shape how the individual views certain practices and also what they value. For example, the Hispanic culture is currently one of the few cultures that has sustained higher birth rates. Many people of Spanish descent value large families and it is a big part of their culture. Their sustained higher birth rates have been maintained even in a global environment where overall birth rate has been steadily declining for the past thirty years.

It is important that we recognize that generations, communication, personalities and culture all need to be factored into our interactions with the people we work with. I am thinking of a recent meeting I had with a Russian entrepreneur. He has been in Canada for more than ten years but his accent is still very heavy. He speaks great English but I left my meeting with extra respect for him because English is his second language. In many ways people who have English as a second language have had to work twice as hard to get to where they are simply by having to think in their own language and translate to English, all in a split second.

Let's look at some of the values of the following cultures and how these values might shape the behaviors of an individual. Even these are not completely true for all of the people within a culture because there are subcultures within cultures. For example, the thoughts and behaviors of someone born and raised in LA would be different from someone born and raised in New York. The examples below are generalized cultural norms associated with each of the cultures but in no means are they true for all groups within these cultures. We could even call them stereotypes but that is not my intent here. My intent is to point out "global" perceptions around each culture to help us understand them better.

Asian: family-oriented, polite and passive, respects authority, hard working, fears letting their family down.

British: monarchists, cynical, suspicious, gossips, hard working, proper, professional.

Canadian: polite, friendly, multiculturally aware, humble, down to earth.

American: bold, risk takers, energetic, success oriented, dreamers.

German: strict, abrupt, opinionated, authoritarian, hard working.

What cultural awareness gives us is insight into another of the factors (along with gender, generation and personality) that make the person who they are and helps us to understand why they do what they do. The most enlightened leaders are those who are able to see the whole person, respect them for who they are and therefore want to help people succeed to their highest level possible.

39: LANGUAGE

The way we speak to each other creates either positive feelings or negative feelings. It was Maya Angelou who said, "It's not what you say or do, it's how you make people feel." Well, I agree with her that it is how you make people feel, but how you talk to people can greatly affect how they feel.

In a previous chapter we talked about personality types and how using what we know about personalities can make a huge difference when communicating. Many people feel that they are good communicators and yet they still find themselves misunderstood or not getting the results they would like with the people with whom they communicate.

It comes down to how we use language. The words we choose and the intent we have when speaking those words can greatly influence how the other person receives what is being said. We all know that in communication there is a sender and a receiver. We also know that everyone's perceptions are real—in other words, their perceptions are real for them.

Modern communication theory suggests that we also tune in to what is not being said to infer meaning from body language, emotional response and word use.

To demonstrate how far we have come with communication, remember the days when "good communication" was using assertive language? Today it is not about using assertive sentences as much as using a form of "win-win" language. It is a more sophisticated and a more intuitive way of communicating and it creates relationships more quickly because the people involved are connected by authenticity.

The language of a Gen Y is often full of acronyms such as:

LOL: laugh out loud

ROFL: rolling on the floor laughing

? U@: where are you at?

To connect with Gen Y we need to be speaking their language. Their language also includes nicknames, something I mentioned earlier in the book. In the workplace we want to be using language that is positive, future focused and yet accountable with Gen Y.

An example of communication to a Gen Y might be, "Good job, Stephen! You have really improved in your phone answering skills. For the future we want to make sure we mention the warranty—this is where we make our money. You tend to rush the person and forget the warranty. Right now you are at zero; I would like to see you at five mentions before the end of the day."

If you were a Gen Y communicating with a Zoomer you need to speak the language of the Zoomer. You could say something like, "Boss, it seems like you have worked really hard to get where you are. I can't even begin to understand the commitment and time you have put into your job. I just can't see myself being here for ten years before I get an opportunity to move up. What would I have to demonstrate to you over the next six months that would get me closer to the promotion I am looking for? What are realistic steps that would let me get to where I want to go?"

An example of a Gen X communicating to a Gen Y might be, "Hey, Sam! I know how it is—you want to get the job done so you can get out early and go skiing with your friends. I totally respect that. Here's what I need from you before I can let you go and have fun. I need you to get your call list done and I need your report on the customer service technology that you promised would be done today. If you can get those to me by, say, four PM you are free to go, my friend."

An example of a Gen X communicating to a Zoomer: "Hey, boss, I know you get so frustrated with our Gen Ys and I can understand your frustration. Here's the bottom line. We can't make them work the way we would and so I have come up with creative incentives to get the work done. For example, I just told Sam that if he got me his customer service technology report and had his call list done by four he could take off and go skiing. It's 4:05 and he got it to me so he is off to ski. Leave it to me, boss."

With Gen X you need to focus on bottom line, on time and we are doing fine! Get to the point—use fast and short language.

With Zoomers recognize the work, show the process and state what's happening next.

Language is also becoming a huge issue in the global workplace. Technology is available to translate nearly any language into your dominant language on a PDA and I believe we will see more language translation technology being used in the next few years.

If you have other languages in your company you can show your respect and honor for that by learning some key words and phrases in that language to share with your teammates. This shows care for their language and that you are willing to make the effort to learn it on their behalf.

As we move forward, more mixed language in the workplace is going to be the norm and our level of adaptability will have to be high to make communication work.

40: Childcare

Here's a shout out to all of the Gen Xers reading this section. You have a family; you are looking to have it all and balance it all. In the new book *What's Next, Gen X* by Tamara Erickson, she posits that the next decade is for Gen X and that a lot of what Gen X needs and wants will be met by employers recognizing the value of this smaller demographic.

The future of work for employers includes taking into account what stage of life each generation is in and how they can fit family obligations in with their work.

Many companies have gotten quite savvy about providing childcare options for their employees. Take Abbott Pharmaceuticals as an example—it has on-site daycare at its headquarters, plus discounts at regional and national childcare facilities along with free resources and parental support. During the summer the firm offers a camp and a volunteer program for kids in the sixth to ninth grades.

At Accenture a quarter of all employees have children under the age of twelve and the firm provides resources to help locate care. It also has a toll free back-up care hotline for childcare help that costs just $2 to $4 an hour. If workers need to have a friend or relative look after their child in an emergency situation they are eligible for a $50.00 reimbursement.

And then there's Aflac. It has two daycare centers at its headquarters that serve 523 children, more than any other corporate site in Georgia. It also offers outstanding educational options. Toddlers study language, science, culture and music. Older kids learn Spanish and attend dance classes. Aflac also offers childcare subsidies of $150.00 for staff in other locations.

Other companies that have fantastic childcare options are Allstate, American Express, Astra Zeneca and Avon. And that's just the As!

Gen X wants their kids involved with programs offered through their work and they love perks for their kids as well. That's why companies that offer special programs or educational opportunities for kids rank very high on the list for Gen X, or for any generation that has children.

41: Aging Parents

Zoomers are feeling the pressure of having Gen Ys in their twenties still living at home to deal with as well as aging parents. Companies that recognize the stress this creates and provide stress solutions create happy Zoomers. When dealing with aging parents it is hard to know what resources are available. Often the Zoomer feels powerless to deal with a parent who is now becoming more like a dependent child.

My husband, Reg, and I have felt such pressure when my father-in-law passed away in December of 2008 and my husband's mother was widowed. We worried about whether she would make meals for herself or if she would properly take her medication. When we convinced her to move to assisted living it was a blessing but it is still stressful, taking her to her doctor appointments and interacting with the care facility to make sure she is okay.

I am self-employed so there was less stress for me than for Reg, who works for a big corporation. He was trying to fit in calls to his mom's doctor between meetings. Many Zoomers are reluctant to let their employers know that they are struggling with this issue because they come from the school of "no complaints."

Bayer recognized the importance of providing support for this concern by creating the Sandwich Generation Employee Networking Group last year at corporate headquarters in Pittsburgh. The group provides support to a growing number of employees who are sandwiched between raising children and caring for elderly parents at the same time. These individuals meet frequently to discuss family matters like child and elder care, and raising teenagers.

You can bet, though, that both Gen X and Gen Y will use whatever resources will be made available for them to deal with this issue in the future.

Here is a list of resources if you are currently facing the challenge of caring for an elderly parent:

Web sites

http://www.aging-parents-and-elder-care.com
http://www.ehow.com/how_2145292_help-elderly-parent.html
http://www.agingcare.com/

Books

Are Your Parents Driving You Crazy?: Getting to Yes with Competent Aging, Joseph A. Ilardo and Carole R. Rothman, 2005, VanderWyk & Burnham.

The Caregiver's Survival Handbook: How to Care for Your Aging Parent, Alexis Abramson and Mary Anne Dunkin, 2004, Perigee.

You and Your Aging Parent: A Family Guide to Emotional, Social, Health, and Financial Problems, Barbara Silverstone, Helen Kandel Hyman, Kim Waller, Bob Morris and Penny Schwartz, 2008, Oxford University Press.

42: Meetings

Have you ever sat in a meeting and thought that it was a complete waste of time? If you are a Zoomer you know that meetings have been a part of corporate cultures for decades, but Gen X and Y are shifting the way we have meetings as well as the norms for how to behave in a meeting. In large corporations back-to-back meetings are standard, especially if you are in management at any level. As a communications expert I feel that face-to-face meetings are great tools to increase understanding and keep everyone on the same page. But meetings don't work if it seems, at the end of the meeting, that nothing has been accomplished.

Today generational differences are causing some challenges in meetings because of differing expectations of acceptable behavior. Let's take a look at each generation's perception of how meetings should be conducted. Here's Gen Y's take:

- ✓ Want fun and inclusion
- ✓ Want it to be an informal gathering
- ✓ Food is a bonus
- ✓ Want access to their PDAs to take notes and search for information during the meeting
- ✓ Want technology in the presentation, including high-resolution graphics and animation
- ✓ Want to be able to jump in to ask questions and interact.

Gen X's perfect meeting looks a little different:

- ✓ Want there to be a tangible outcome to the meeting
- ✓ Want the meeting to be short
- ✓ Want the data needed to make a decision to be at the meeting

- ✓ Want updates on actions taken after last meeting
- ✓ Will leave the room to take a call on their BlackBerry
- ✓ Want to bring their laptop to the meeting to take notes.

Zoomers are different again:

- ✓ Like to hold meetings; they see it as face time
- ✓ Expect others to meet when it is convenient for their schedule—want to meet at their preferred time of day
- ✓ Want to assign teams to tasks, expect follow-up reports
- ✓ Like to use whiteboards and flip charts
- ✓ Bring notebooks to take notes and then transfer notes to an e-mail or Word document
- ✓ Turn off their PDAs to stay focused on the presenter and the meeting.

As you can see, each generation sees meetings from their own perspective. I don't think that any of these ways are better than the others. When I speak I am used to seeing people with their PDAs and I don't see it as rude. I see it as their way of taking notes or tweeting. I see the future of meetings as even more virtual in the future because of technology. Face-to-face meetings will become much more focused, with tighter timeframes. Some suggestions to make the meeting appeal to all the generations are:

- ✓ Open with a fun icebreaker relevant to the content of the meeting
- ✓ Outline the expectations for the meeting, such as "turn off your PDAs," in advance
- ✓ Use technology to present and keep information on slides short and sweet
- ✓ Provide an agenda both by e-mail and at the meeting, posted on a flip chart, whiteboard or slide
- ✓ Talk about accomplishments since the last meeting to show action has been taken
- ✓ Allow interaction and exchange of ideas among everyone present. If time does not allow for this to be done verbally, get them to write ideas or thoughts on sticky notes and have them compiled after the meeting
- ✓ Follow up the meeting with assigned action items, deadlines and commitments.

43: WELLNESS

It may seem like a tall order, but for a few businesses focusing on health and wellness has gone a long way to make employees happier. Employees from all of the generations are looking for companies focused on health and wellbeing. Below are some examples of what companies are offering in regards to health and wellness.

The Rhein Chemie chemicals company in Chardon OH customizes additives and specialties for the rubber, lubricant and plastics industries. "We participated in a survey of the best companies to work for. We haven't gotten results back yet, but our company is interested in how they're perceived as an employer and want this place to be a good place to work," the CEO said. "The economy made it rough, but we're also trying to take the steps to keep people happy and make this a fun place to work and for people to want to come in and do their job."

To keep its employees engaged, Rhein Chemie has a wellness program that includes physicals, flu shots, a fitness membership reimbursement program, a mini-triathlon, a "biggest loser" contest and a health fair, according to the company. "We also have a Weight Watchers at Work program," the CEO said. "There's a core group of people that do that. They love it. They get together once a week and have a meeting." The group meets to discuss goals and keep each other motivated, the CEO said, adding if the employees hit their goal, at the end of the twelve-week program the company pays the membership fee. "We do different employee luncheons that the company sponsors if we have a good performance," the CEO said.

As another fitness-related incentive, a Thousand-Mile Club gives a gift card to people who record 1000 miles of activity by the end of the year. "They can do a combination of running, biking, walking, jogging," the CEO said. "Employees get together in groups and they can go out together after work or at lunch and walk up and down Park Court here. It's good because it gets them to interact with each other." Participants are on an honor system, but they are also provided with logbooks to keep track of their miles and can enter certain activities into the fitness reimbursement program database as well.

PolyChem Corporation of Mentor OH, which manufactures plastic strapping for the packing industry, was also hit with layoffs and cutbacks last year but has still not lost its health focus. It engaged its employees in a weight-loss competition called "Lose It for Good." "Before, the team that lost the most weight would win and they got individually rewarded. This year, the new twist is that everyone creates a team and the company will donate the total amount of pounds lost by all of the teams in food to a food bank," said Anne Webb, human resources manager for the company.

Another Ohio employer, The UH Geauga Medical Center, is part of the University Hospitals group. It takes advantage of a few University Hospitals programs but also creates some of its own on a more local level. The medical center's employee rewards and recognition committee, composed of employees selected by managers of each department, serves as a human barometer for the company to gauge what elements of the system are working well and what could use improvement.

"Employees get extremely involved in the process," marketing manager Lou Ann Marx said. "We also initiated last year a 'Hero of the Month' program. An employee who goes above and beyond is selected each month… and voted on by their peers. That's been successful." University Hospitals Geauga Medical Center also recently started an employee forum, which has served as a way for the medical center's president, Steven Jones, to communicate with the staff and give updates about where the company is and where they hope to go, Marx said. On top of the annual employee picnic, holiday lunch and pancake breakfast—where all the department heads serve their employees— the President's Awards are also given out. "That's where three stellar employees are selected by the president," Marx said, adding that the directors and managers of each department make the nominations. Melody Obery, manager of human resources, added the medical center also participates in the UH recognition platform, which is an online tool that gives out thank yous to employees who go above and beyond. "We're really trying to create a culture of appreciation in what we do and how we do it," Obery said. "We have a lot of executive involvement. They like to see, touch and feel the people that are helping the organization."

The effort to create team spirit among employees is reflected in the amount of volunteering that takes place every year, Marx said. "We have a tent up at the Geauga County Fair every year and we have over 100 employees volunteer each year," she said. "They want to attend. You don't find that just anywhere. I really think Geauga Hospital is a family. The employees realize that we're in hard times. The economy has impacted everyone and they work together as a team."

As you can tell with the examples provided above, companies recognize the value of keeping their employees alive and well.

44: Succession Planning

Many people think that succession planning is a top-down activity involving management and seasoned professionals. It is better to involve Gen X and Y as well so that they can help create a vision that involves all of the generations in a company.

If you think of succession planning as a continual process, one way to involve Gen Ys is to hold regular meetings with junior employees (professional staff), invite them to ask questions during the meeting and listen to their input. By tapping into group wisdom at all levels, partners, shareholders, executives and managers can discover a lot about what can make their companies more successful and what the most important attributes are that the company needs to foster. After all, the Gen Ys have a longer future ahead of them and they see and experience the world in different ways. By engaging them in this important activity, the organization will be more likely to retain their best talent.

Managers and supervisors should be looking for leadership attributes among the Gen Ys. Managers need to allow Gen Ys the chance to volunteer for or take on responsibility for significant internal projects. That way they will have a chance to prove themselves beyond their technical competencies.

Professionalism is an important concern in the succession and transition process in many respects. Will successors treat clients in the most professional manner: in communication, behavior, prompt attention to their concerns, privacy, confidentiality and ethics?

An effective transition process requires professional development of the Gen Y in client relationship management. Members of Gen Y may not have learned the interpersonal and relationship-building skills necessary at home, in school or during most companies' typical training programs. Often they don't realize what is missing. They only know what they have been taught and usually are too busy to seek the coaching they need on their own. Managers need to make sure this training or coaching is provided.

To foster effective transitions, companies need to create an environment attractive to Gen X, Y and Zoomer generations. It can be built around what people of all generations want: to be respected, recognized, and remembered. They also want to be coached, consulted on actions that will affect them, and connected to their organization and its mission.

Steps to generational succession planning:
1. Identify roles that require succession planning
2. Create key areas with measurements for tasks within the roles to be filled
3. Identify Gen X and Y employees who have a natural cultural "fit"
4. Identify talent attributes and training gaps
5. Provide training and mentoring
6. Mentor them through client relationships and leadership projects
7. Provide feedback and identify further training gaps
8. Rate key competencies of the role on a scale of one to ten for the roles to be filled
9. Promote the Gen X and Y to leadership positions.

45: REWARDS

When we hear "years of service" we think of grandfather clocks and crystal vases. Perhaps that worked in the past but not with the Gen Y generation. The companies that are using the recession to drop reward programs may want to rethink that decision.

We are now in a knowledge-based economy where innovation and information give organizations a competitive edge. This knowledge-based economy depends on the knowledge-based worker, who can be characterized as diverse, creative, and one who no longer stays with one company their entire career.

In fact, in 2008, the average employee tenure was 4.1 years. Statistics reveal that the typical Generation Y member will have had ten jobs by the age of thirty-eight and stay an average of 1.5 years with each employer (source: US Department of Labor's Bureau of Labor Statistics). Generation Y employees will represent 40 percent of the workforce in five years.

Unfortunately, despite the changes in the working world, in the workforce and in most other human resources practices, service award programs have remained virtually unchanged, says Razor Suleman, CEO and founder of I Love Rewards (www.iloverewards.com). Most companies still wait to reward and recognize at the standard intervals—five, ten, fifteen and twenty years.

Companies who wait to reward risk losing their top talent and miss the opportunity to engage their employees, particularly Generation Y employees who have grown up to expect easy recognition. Too many companies offer "too little too late" in terms of rewards and recognition!

While antiquated service and recognition programs cost companies employees by failing to recognize achievements fast enough, it may cost them potential employees as well, says Suleman. He suggests that many top performers will look at an antiquated recognition program and wonder what else in the company is equally outdated or ineffective.

Suleman notes that while some companies dispensed with their service award programs completely during the economic downturn over the past year, he has found that many more have not only continued their programs but have developed some novel approaches.

Suleman points to the following trends in particular:

- ✓ Companies are offering awards with increasing frequency. Instead of waiting for five years of service, many companies are starting to realize that a first year of completed service deserves recognition as well. One company, a large brewery, gives its first-anniversary employees a beer stein complete with a toast and a speech to celebrate the anniversary.
- ✓ Peer-to-peer recognition. At I Love Rewards, peers can recognize when a co-worker makes a contribution or reinforces company values by awarding 500 points. Each point is only worth a cent (so 500 points equals $5.00), but these points can be accumulated and added to other reward points, which are then subsequently redeemed on something the employee chooses.
- ✓ Still recognizing the traditional milestones. However, now there are options that allow employees to decide what types of recognition, or gift items, they receive.

Suleman notes that Gen Yers have grown up in affluent times, conditioned by their parents and society to be rewarded—often merely for participating. Now that it is entering the workforce, however, this new generation is quickly learning the need to perform. Still, Gen Ys look to tangible rewards, such as praise and gift items, to confirm that performance.

How can organizations tailor years of service award programs to the needs of business and employees today? Transform them with the following three best practices. Offer employees the rewards and recognition that inspire innovation and strengthen employee alignment with the organization.

1. Focus on recognition first, then reward. Most companies spend a large portion of their human resources budget on years of service programs because they want the reward to be valuable and well-received. Companies need to realize that it's not the money spent but the recognition the employee receives. Recognition makes people feel valued, and an employee who feels valued is more likely to be motivated and engaged.

2. Offer rewards that make an impact. Just as recognition should be personal, so should the reward. Many options are available today that allow employees to choose their own rewards. One option is moving to a points-based currency where employees are awarded points and can redeem them for items of their choice.

Incentive trips are still being used by organizations in Canada. Home Hardware regularly takes its store owners (who pay for their own trips) to an exotic destination, where they attend meetings but also have time to spend with their spouses and families in a location they might not have visited without the company's help. The corporate office pays for the meeting activities but all attendees get to mix business with pleasure. It creates great loyalty to the Home Hardware brand and culture.

Other popular employee rewards include the latest and greatest in personal electronics, experiential rewards for adventure seekers and the ability to donate the monetary value of the reward to the charity of their choice. The benefit to providing choice is that employees feel their employer is empowering them to choose the reward that best fits their individual lifestyle and needs.

3. Automate the system. The two most common nuisances associated with organizing traditional service awards are administration and reward redemption headaches. Traditional programs are painfully slow to process and involve a great deal of manual work. Look for a system that will handle the administrative aspects for you—and make the program rewarding for HR as well.

The future of years of service awards is here. Tailoring the program to your organization and the needs of your employees will help you build a culture of recognition, not of entitlement, in your workplace.

46: TEAM RECOGNITION

The days of "one size fits all" in regards to team recognition are over. You can't just have a Pizza Friday and expect that everyone will view that as a great reward. Many Zoomers reading this will remember that just having food brought in for a meeting was a bonus. In Chapter Twenty Seven we talked about recognition for each individual but many companies are seeing the benefits of team recognition. This appeals specifically to Gen Y who flourishes in a team environment and also likes to celebrate success with a team.

The most important aspect of team recognition is to ensure it is done in such a way that the team appreciates it. For example, a Gen Y team would be totally thrilled if you made a YouTube video giving them praise and then e-mailed it or posted it to the company web site for everyone to see. Or if you created a picture montage of the team, put it to music and posted it to Facebook.

On the other hand, a Zoomer team would be more thrilled with a team bonus or reward. A Gen X team would want you to "show them the money," give them a team outing away from the office or give them tickets to a sporting event that the whole team gets to attend.

One way to measure team performance is to look at goals. The goals based approach would base team bonuses on a combination of financial results and other ratios. Possible measurements include:

- ✓ Customer retention rate.
- ✓ New customers.
- ✓ Customer satisfaction.
- ✓ 360 degree performance evaluation results for the team.
- ✓ On time delivery.

- ✓ Project cycle times.
- ✓ Team innovations.

As Tom Peters puts it, "Provide bold financial incentives for everyone. Incentive pay for team performance is the 'clincher,' the ultimate recognition for a contribution to improved company performance." He's absolutely right! A productive company providing superior services and sharing its success with its employees is a team that is hard to beat.

47: Social Media

Generation Y is the fastest-growing segment of the North American workforce today. This is a generation whose behavior and worldview is dominated by two factors that pull them in different directions: technology and anxiety. Whenever I bring up social media in front of an audience I get the Zoomers in the audience groaning when I talk about Facebook and other social networking options.

Zoomers feel they don't need any more friends and they find online networking tiresome. Having said this, Zoomers do use Facebook, as do Gen Xs, but more for connecting with existing family and friends. The fact that you can share photos, video and so much more is what draws all users to Facebook.

My daughter Courtney and I often use Facebook instant messaging to talk to each other; I can also see what she is up to as she posts pictures and updates her status. It helps me feel like I know what's going on with her since she no longer lives at home.

The Gen Ys in the audience love social media because they are an always-on, always-connected generation, and consequently the line between work and private life has begun to blur. I mentioned previously in the book that technology was the major factor changing the rules of work for Gen Y.

Gen Ys believe in the power of social media. They demonstrate their belief in a variety of ways including social networks. One of these involves a sense of belonging developed in online communities and the personal branding that the communities inevitably foster. With technology, Gen Y makes connections across borders, gender, race, religion and sexual orientation.

MySpace, Facebook, Twitter, and Flickr allow a person to create a personal brand, something that was never possible for previous generations. YouTube's tagline is "Broadcast Yourself," and members create and protect their personal brands in the same ways that business marketers create and protect their product brands.

Another network effect involves the almost-instantaneous "viral" spread of information among Gen Ys. Information today moves like the flu through online networks and opinions are sorted out in the process. Information is quickly sized up and deemed to be good or bad, useful or useless, cool or uncool. The wisdom of groups rules the process, as music, politics, gossip, clothing and beliefs all pass through the network and are judged at high speed. A message must be attractive and considered innovative by the masses to make it through the process. Facebook, with over 60 million users, gets a significant amount of Gen Y attention. More than half of Facebook users are in the eighteen to twenty-four age groups, according to comScore Inc. research.

Since Facebook is also one of the ten most visited web sites in the United States, it is not a surprise that companies large and small are now taking steps to create presences on Facebook for recruiting purposes. To build a successful recruiting program on social networking sites like Facebook, you must respect the unwritten rules of Gen Y. This generation expects you to respect their community, and they are not concerned with traditional hierarchies of power and authority. They don't respond to traditional marketing, but instead to authenticity and understanding.

Their attention span is short because they are constantly moving from one idea or trend to the next, and they will not stay with an employer unless the employer provides them with a variety of experiences. Keep them moving. One theory about why information technology (IT) has lost its charm for college students is that the IT industry actually consists of 150 different jobs practiced in relative isolation. Gen Y prefers collaboration and teamwork. If you want to attract Gen Y candidates to replace retiring Zoomers or Zoomers who are cutting back their hours, start by structuring jobs for interaction and teamwork and defining career paths with variety in mind.

Gen Y is a unique generation. Technology and networking has bred them to be comfortable in a world of speedy global networks where decisions about adopting or discarding ideas are made faster than ever before. On the other hand, coming into adulthood in post-9/11 America has made them more needy for community and security than their parents were at their age. Looming social and political crises are a threat to their way of life. Social media has created a sense of belonging, community and identity for Gen Y.

The opportunities for Zoomers, Gen X and Gen Y are to look at innovative ways to use social media to increase business, reach the Gen Y group for research or recruiting and look at direct applications of social media in the workplace.

48: Job Titles

Zoomers have worked in companies where job titles held and still hold cachet. In contrast, Gen X has gotten a little jaded with job titles—they realize that a new job title can simply mean they have been placated so that they will stick around a little longer. Gen Y does not have much of an attachment to job titles. They really don't care what you call them as long as they are getting paid to have fun at work while having time for their personal life too.

Just for fun I searched for job titles posted on Craigslist and found the following:

PlayStation Brand Ambassador
Eyebrow Threader
Finish Carpenter
Nail Tech
Remedy Engineer
Saltlick Cashier
Breakfast Sandwich Maker
Glacéau Drop Team
DoodyCalls Technician
Golf Staff
Pressure Washers
Sandwich Artist
Self Storage Manager
Qualified Infant Caregiver
Ground Support
Commercial Space Hunter
Job Coach

Kids Kamp Instructor

Pools Supervisor

House Manager/Teen Supervisor.

Seriously, though, organizations like Google have some pretty cool job titles that are appealing to Gen Y, such as Social Media Technician. A friend of mine owns a marketing company and she has very interesting job titles for her staff, like Chief Website Artist. Some big organizations have positions such as Chief Happiness Officer. My editor Kedre's dad worked for GM all of his life and he used to have a saying, "Title in lieu of salary." Every time they changed his job title they had him order new business cards. One time for a joke he got cards listing him as "vice-president of empty boxes."

Standard job titles are being replaced with more creative and hip titles to make them more appealing to both Gen X and Gen Y.

The company I am currently working with is re-vamping all of its job titles and job descriptions with input from their Gen Y employees. They are a smaller company so getting input from all staff is more viable than for a larger corporation.

The trend for unique job titles will continue within the next five years as the Gen Ys move to become 40 percent of the workforce. If you're a Zoomer, get ready to have some pretty funky titles!

49: EDUCATION

One of the hottest benefits being offered on the job market today is education. Not only does it help attract the best and the brightest applicants, but it also ensures that a company's workforce continuously maintains its edge over competitors. Zoomers see the value in continuing their education and many have gotten their MBAs or other degrees while working full time. Their company pays for their tuition or a portion thereof and the Zoomer employee puts in the time and effort to obtain the degree.

Not everyone wants a formal degree, so there are a variety of education options. Progressive companies recognize there are many alternative types of education such as diploma programs.

Here's a look at what each of the generations are looking for in regards to education:

Gen Y wants you to provide education related to doing their jobs but also wants you to pay for their continuing education. A good portion of Gen Ys recognize the value of college and university degrees and they are looking for companies willing to pay for all or a portion of their courses in diploma programs, college programs or university degrees.

Many Gen Xs are going back to school while working, to get their MBA, CPA or equivalent professional degree in their fields. They are looking for financial reimbursement but they are also looking at time off to write a thesis or a sabbatical to complete a difficult university program. They are also looking for time to do schoolwork—maybe coming in a little later in the morning so that they can write a paper or study.

The Zoomer is going through a reinvention phase. Many already have an MBA or a degree but they know they must keep their education up to date and relevant. They are asking to go on educational retreats such as the ones being offered by Harvard University, one-week or two-week certification programs in specific fields. They are asking the companies they work for to fund this element of their continued learning.

To remain competitive companies need to look at paying for education as a necessary expense related to attracting and retaining high performing employees. Think of your investment in your employees' education as an investment in your company's results. Yes, they may leave after you have paid for their schooling but consider that every other company is expected to do the same. It is your contribution to the employee "pool" I talked about in a previous chapter.

50: COMPENSATION

"Are you ready for this generation and the next?" It's a question on the mind of any executive wanting to capture the talent of Generation X and younger employees to maintain a competitive edge. But determining the best benefits and compensation solutions to motivate current and prospective employees can be a challenge.

Companies have been talking about "pay for performance" for over a decade and many companies have successfully made the necessary changes to become performance-focused enterprises. However, the past few years of a tougher economy have shown many companies that they were merely "talking the talk" of being performance focused. Sheer economics and employee engagement statistics point to the need to be "walking the talk" on performance focused compensation.

A consulting client that I have mentioned earlier, Care Pest, is an example of a company that has had to look at how it recognizes performance and compensates for performance. The company realized that setting targets and hoping the business will come is no longer a sustainable way of being in business, and that sales-focused behavior needs to come from all members of the company. The owners sat down with their management team and communicated the shift to a performance-based focus and what that meant. It meant that compensation would be tied to deliverables and goals achieved.

The gap between the twenty-somethings of Generation Y and the thirty-somethings of Generation X demonstrates more than a difference in age. It represents distinct differences in taste and priority. The thirty-somethings of Generation X, for instance, are known for being the generation that is having families and increasing the number of mothers in the workplace. The twenty-somethings of Generation Y are thought to be "demanding, impatient and bad at communicating" by some (from a 2007 survey of business owners in Australia). Paper-based processes and defined benefits plans may have worked for the Baby Boomer generation, but younger employees expect online access and greater compensation options for themselves and their families as they mature.

Bryan Bach is director of HR for Pie Town Productions, which develops reality and documentary programming such as *House Hunters* and *Design on a Dime*. He said Pie Town has a young employee base and is a heavily e-mail-driven organization.

To appeal to the younger generations, companies realize they need online communication to enable résumé submissions, benefits podcasts, employee testimonials and online job finding tools.

Bach learned that offering online access to employee benefits was a natural extension of adopting self-service to simplify benefits management for HR, one that brought greater employee satisfaction, accessibility and choice.

"When I pulled the plug on the paper system for online enrollment, people jumped on it," he said. "Sometimes it takes them five minutes, ten minutes, and they are done. They can do it at home, over the weekend. It gives them a lot of flexibility."

While younger employees sometimes understand technology faster than those in older age groups, all employees benefit from the company's online enrollment and management system, said Jan Coulman. Coulman is in charge of HR at Ubisoft, a leading international developer, publisher and distributor of gaming and other products, such as "Rayman" and "Tom Clancy's Splinter Cell."

Benefits updates and company news are posted regularly on the company intranet, and employees are notified by e-mail in advance of important events, such as open enrollment. A one-page action guide describes updates for the year, along with cost and benefits changes and includes a "cheat sheet" with the steps to enroll or make changes.

There is even new technology that can automatically communicate the complete cost of employee compensation. The cost to maintain that employee, including an itemization of salary and all benefits offered, can be automatically presented when employees log in. This can be an eye-opener for all generations, but especially for those who are younger and less familiar with the cost of benefit plans. This helps talent managers "sell" their company's offerings. Talent managers can also solicit feedback on benefit plans offered through online portals or post surveys to determine if offerings are meeting employee needs.

Regardless of the company's current composition, the challenge for executives is identifying the needs of the existing workforce and determining how to persuade future talent to bring their skills to the organization. Having greater access to information about current and proposed workforces and potential benefits options is critical when developing effective compensation and benefits programs. Technology can help talent managers find answers and communicate important information to management and employees using the methods that the Gen Ys prefer.

CHERYL CRAN

51: Project Management

Zoomers will recall that it was not that long ago that a printed Project Plan would mark the start of any project. The key stakeholders would physically sign the document, which would be passed among parties in the internal mail, finally returning to the project manager to update the document to version 1.0. He or she would then file it away for safekeeping and proof that the initiation phase was over and that the real work could begin. Does that sound like your workplace now?

Most Gen X and some Zoomer project leaders would now expect the entire approvals process to be done by e-mail. That is not to say that you can skip getting formal project approval. Instead, the way you go about securing sign-off is different because of the technology available to you—and them—in the workplace. No longer do project managers have a filing cabinet of original functional specs and documents signed off in ink. Managers are more likely to have limited storage space for project files. They probably store files electronically on a central shared server, with scanned copies of any documentation that has been signed. Copies of approval e-mails are archived with the rest of the project documents. This is now the accepted way of working, even in industries like financial services, which typically take a while to catch up.

This approach to handling project documentation has evolved with the availability of technology at work, and in the way we use it. This has given rise to the "Google generation." You probably fall into this category. It does not have to do with age. It is a distinction based on the adoption of new technology.

If you want information, you can go to Google (or your favorite search engine), type in your question and get a relevant response in a fraction of a second. The Google search engine has changed the way project stakeholders expect to get information. In other words, if you need to find something out you expect to be able to do so quickly and conveniently. It is no longer necessary to trawl through books or manuals or take a trip to the library to do research. If you don't know the answer, you can Google the question on your computer or mobile phone.

In the past—and it wasn't that long ago—the monthly steering group report would be an adequate representation of a project's status. Everyone acknowledged that it was not a real-time project position, but it was accurate enough for the purposes of judging progress against milestones and budget. This data would be sufficient for the steering group, and if anyone else wanted a formal project status report, the latest steering group report could be handed over as a snapshot in time. Most of the time people were happy with this level of detail, even though they knew it could no longer be true. Only in an emergency would any one ask to see anything more up to date.

Today, project stakeholders have different expectations about project information because they can get other information at the click of button. You want to know the weather in Bangalore? Google it. You want real-time stock prices on the FTSE? Google them. You want up to date project status reports? Here's last month's steering group report, precisely nineteen days out of date. Well, no. This lack of real-time data is no longer acceptable to project stakeholders who can get everything else in a fraction of a second.

Sixteen percent of the workforce is what research group IDG calls hyper-connected. These people have "fully embraced the brave new world… They liberally use technological devices and applications for both personal and business use." IDG also estimates that the number of workers falling into this category could soon be up to 40 percent.

Best Buy has something called "Tag Trade" that allows project managers to post their projects on the main server and other project stakeholders can comment on or rate the progress of the project—this gives a whole new meaning to keeping people in the loop.

The fact that people are connected at work and at home has a knock-on impact on the way in which we provide project data. Now project stakeholders expect real-time, up to date status reports. At the very least they expect you to give them that information whenever they ask for it, by return e-mail. Project managers now have to deal with those raised expectations and must always be on top of project status in case anyone asks.

And I think we should be. Project managers who don't know what is going on—and are not able to communicate it—aren't serving the needs of the project team or the wider stakeholder community.

52: PHILANTHROPY

Zoomers have been socially conscious since they were teenagers. They would argue that they were environmentally concerned long before the current trend. The Zoomers who lived through the '60s were socially conscious until they became adults and the consumer bug bit them—then they wanted to have more material wealth than their frugal Traditionalist parents.

Today philanthropy is on everyone's mind regardless of his or her generation, but increasingly Gen Y is looking for companies doing something big and wonderful, either in the local community or globally.

A friend of mine, David Gouthro, is a consultant. His daughter Anna would be considered a Millennial and she is a great example of philanthropy at a young age. She recently held an event at her school to raise money for families in Haiti—they raised $300.00. Gen Y and Millenials are globally aware and because of technology in the school environment they are connected to global events every moment of the day.

Another colleague of mine, Tim Sanders, wrote the book *Saving the World at Work*. In it he talks about the competitive advantages gained by organizations focused on doing good in the world.

Recently I worked with Home Hardware in Canada, a very big community contributor. In addition to corporate-level contributions, storeowners are invited to an annual conference where part of the agenda is business and the rest is building homes as part of Habitat for Humanity. This has become an annual event that the home office and storeowners look forward to attending. One person I spoke to who had been on the last trip to Mexico to help build homes said that she and her husband were so moved that it helped them inspire their own store to get involved with Habitat for Humanity at the local level.

Gen X and Gen Y are cynical of organizations that are focused on profits alone. They are keen on working with companies who are focused on making a global difference with a cause. Consider the following Gen Y's comments on philanthropy:

"I don't consider myself a philanthropist, because I don't give away very much money. What I give is time," said Katherine Lorenz, a self-described "workaholic" and co-founder of a nonprofit organization that partners with rural communities in Mexico to promote better nutrition and health. Puente a la Salud Comunitaria, the organization Lorenz established and now directs, centers on an unusual entry point to community empowerment: the re-introduction of an ancient and highly nutritious grain, amaranth, into the diet of the largely indigenous, rural poor population of Oaxaca.

At twenty-eight years of age Katherine is a Gen Y who avidly wants to make a difference and works extremely hard because she believes in the contributions she is making to the planet.

Sustainable development is also a major focus of her family's philanthropy, and Lorenz is the first member of her generation to serve as a board member on the Cynthia and George Mitchell Foundation, established by her grandparents. Lorenz is trying to establish a next-generation committee to bring the interests of younger family members to the board.

How could your company create Gen Y involvement and leadership in the philanthropic areas of your business? This is an area that creates highly engaged and excited Gen Ys in the workplace. Zoomers and Gen X perceive that they have less time but they too are more excited and engaged with organizations that are giving back to their communities and the globe.

53: Dress Code

This is an interesting topic of discussion when I bring it up in a mixed group of Zoomers, Gen Xs and Ys. Zoomers often express great frustration at Gen Y's "lack of common sense" when it comes to dress code. A lot of Gen Ys I have talked to feel that the way Zoomers and Gen X dress is "stuffy." Many Gen Ys like to dress up once in a while in a dress or a suit but they don't see it as necessary to do every day. Their attitude towards dress reflects their casual attitude about life and work.

Remember, though, that Gen Y is also a generation brought up on sexy role models like Britney Spears and Lady Gaga, and Gen Y ladies do not see the problem with wearing tank tops as opposed to long-sleeved tops.

I remember when my daughter Courtney was in high school the teachers would send kids home if they were wearing "inappropriate" summer clothes. One day Courtney came home indignant because she didn't understand the problem with wearing a tank top in the hot days of spring. Courtney was never one to dress inappropriately so she took extreme offense at being told to change her shirt. When she and I spoke about it I explained to her that a wide-strap tank top with a round neck was probably acceptable but a thin-strap, low-cut tank top would not be. That is my point at work. Zoomers and Gen X need to take the time to offer a "what to wear" list and a "what not to wear" list so that there are clear guidelines on what is acceptable.

One group I worked with a few years ago got very creative with this issue. It was a very large pharmaceutical company and the staff was finding that their Gen Ys were dressing somewhat out of line with the company dress code. Rather than get militant about it they got creative:

they held a "What Not to Wear" fashion show. What was fantastic about their idea is that they had the senior management come out in the "What Not to Wear" examples, which caused major hilarity, but then they had Gen Y staff come out in the "What to Wear" examples.

The results of this creative approach to enforcing the dress code were amazing—the experience inadvertently became a morale booster because everyone was able to have a laugh without feeling singled out. Senior management were able to poke some fun at themselves, which created more levity and relaxation around the issue of the dress code.

Another company uses graphics in a cartoon format in the Human Resources section of their intranet—their internal web site—to show what to wear and what not to wear.

Zoomers or Gen Xs can continue to get frustrated with the supposed lack of common sense regarding dress with Gen Ys or we can get creative and fun with it by establishing guidelines in a fun and humorous way.

54: DIVERSITY

When I grew up on a farm in Saskatchewan in the '60s and '70s we took a bus to school and all of my schoolmates were Caucasian. In fact, I did not get exposure to other cultures until our family moved to the Okanagan in BC when I was a teenager. It was at that stage of my life that I met Indo-Canadians, Asians and people from other cultures. Fast forward to the childhoods of Gen Y and the Millenials: they have never known anything other than being a part of multiple cultures. In school diversity of cultures is honored and it is no longer assumed that all people are Christians or that all people have the same practices or rituals in their homes.

Companies that are more diverse actually have a greater competitive advantage. We have seen in the last decade that companies are looking for people who speak more than one language as business becomes more global instead of strictly serving North America. There is also a growing industry of cross-cultural specialists.

I find it fascinating that diversity is viewed very differently depending on where you go in North America. For example, here in Vancouver we have obvious and accepted multiculturalism but when I travel to other cities and towns there are distinct differences in the levels of acceptance of our country's diversity. I remember speaking in Billings, Montana years ago—they made it very clear to me that visitors were welcome but they didn't want outsiders moving to their community. In fact, many were against Californians purchasing second homes there or moving to Montana because they wanted their state's dominant culture to stay the way it was.

The challenge with wanting to keep the status quo is that eventually it inhibits growth. If we don't have interprovincial or interstate migration we do not benefit from the knowledge, experience and fresh ideas that can help us grow and prosper. The same could be said for immigration. More and more companies are now looking to other countries for employees because many native-born Gen Ys are not interested in physical labor or non-technical work, which has made some occupations unappealing to them. Take construction, for example. It is working hard as an industry to recruit Gen Ys but overall Gen Ys are more attracted to technical work and less to manual labor. Therefore many construction firms are hiring Gen Xs and Zoomers from Europe, where manufacturing and craftsmanship are still a big part of working life. There are even government programs in place to help companies recruit from other regions.

Along with diversity come challenges such as language and religious differences. Many businesses allow for these differences because they recognize the value of honoring ritual and practice for all cultures. For example, companies are coming up with creative ways to educate their staff on the various cultures within their organizations.

A kitchen cabinet company in Toronto has many staff from different countries who speak different languages. The company decided that instead of pushing its employees to attend English as a Second Language (ESL) classes it would bring ESL to the workplace. Every Friday the company holds an ESL session during the lunch hour and brings in food from each of the cultures represented so that everyone is exposed to understanding other cultures, practices and beliefs.

This has turned into a very lucrative exercise for this company. It now has a more devoted team of workers who are speaking better English and who are learning about the various cultures of their co-workers.

The advantage for companies in increasing their diversity is that they increase their competitive advantage. I have a consulting client right now who is Native, a former band chief. He recognizes that industry would benefit from hiring youth from his Native community and he is working to bridge the gap between industry and Native communities. There is huge potential for industry to hire Native workers—the Native culture is a huge untapped source of workers that has been largely ignored by industry up to this point.

55: The Big Picture

It used to be when workers were given a task or asked to do a job, they would not ask any questions nor would they ask for a deeper explanation. For many Zoomers the boss was king and whatever he or she asked them to do they simply did. With Gen X there is a slight bit of rebellion—they insist on more information, and want to be included in some of the discussions about their part in a project. Gen Y is looking for the whole deal: they want the big grand picture and then they want the stories about how they fit into the big grand picture and why their task or job is crucial to the overall puzzle.

For many Zoomers this is one of the most frustrating traits of Gen Y. Zoomers have on-the-job experience and time on their side so often they don't know what it is that they know. They get frustrated when an "in the dark" Gen Y asks them to tell everything they know and then break it down into why it should matter.

As companies make the decision to be more open and congruent with business processes they have to look at communicating in new and different ways that appeal to all of the generations. Zoomers appreciate the big picture as well, but in the past they have simply accepted that they weren't given access to that knowledge. They learned to do their piece of the work in a vacuum. The advantage in Gen Y pushing for "big picture and break it down" language is that every generation gets the benefit.

An evolved leader will have already recognized that Gen Y requires the big picture and the steps involved. Instead of getting frustrated he or she sees the merit in taking the time to provide Gen Y with what they want.

Recently while working with a consulting client I suggested that we have a meeting with the primarily Gen Y office team. I had already facilitated a strategic direction retreat with the managers and was also providing one-on-one coaching for each of the leaders. I kept hearing about their challenges with the all-female Gen Y office team, who were struggling with certain aspects of the job. When we had the meeting, what became immediately apparent was that this team of six young Gen Y ladies had not been given much direction. They were told to do a certain task but there was absolutely no explanation given of the task nor why the task was important to the company.

Once we had the meeting and discussed different generational viewpoints, different personalities and different work styles the Gen Y team felt it had more information and direction. The Gen X leaders began to provide information in ways that the Gen Y could hear. Suddenly the productivity of the team went through the roof and the overall morale of the group went up as well.

One skill the office team needed was to know the area so they could schedule jobs for the road crew. The map they had was on the far wall and was in fine print, so very few of the Gen Y staff were referring to it at all. After the meeting the leaders decided to take the office group out on the road to different municipalities to see the areas they serviced, and then provided them with access to Google maps. By blending the experience of the road trip with access to technology the problem was solved.

We must be willing to provide the big picture often and consistently so everyone can be focused on moving forward.

56: Eco-Friendliness

In the chapter on environment I talked about office environment as well as having a concern for the environment. In this chapter I want to talk about how companies have incorporated eco-friendliness into their businesses in a way that has appeal for all of the generations.

Organizations are recognizing the value of taking measures to ensure their offices are as eco-friendly as possible. There are many ways to do that; one of the easiest is to look at energy savings. Some ways to save on energy in the office are:

- ✓ Install more efficient lighting, and motion-activated lights in the washrooms and other occasionally used rooms like storage rooms
- ✓ Use as much natural lighting as possible with windows, skylights and light tubes
- ✓ Choose Energy Star certified computer equipment
- ✓ Set your computers to use power save mode instead of using screen savers
- ✓ Keep thermostats between sixty-eight and seventy-four degrees F
- ✓ Install low flow toilets
- ✓ Recycle all paper and plastic and shred and recycle confidential documents
- ✓ Encourage the use of reusable bags—if you are in the retail industry create your own
- ✓ Offer information on alternative forms of travel to get to the office

✓ Create a "green" committee to keep communication going about being eco-friendly

Best Buy is a great example of being eco-friendly in regards to transportation for their employees. Vancouver head office employees have the option to take public transit to a central location to catch a Best Buy shuttle bus that takes them to the office in the morning and back again in the late afternoon.

Many companies are now holding "green" meetings where there are no handouts on site—the handouts are offered on a conference web site for uploading. More and more companies are also encouraging their employees to not print their documents, using secure server storage capabilities instead to save paper.

Zoomers have a tough time with not being able to print documents because they are so accustomed to having that piece of paper in their hands. However once Zoomers are confident that they can access the documents they need online from a secure location they tend to make the transition to paperless work more easily. Gen X and Y are so used to storing all of their information on electronic devices that the thought of printing something is outright archaic for them.

Pundits said that when e-mail was created it would reduce paper, but remember that the early adopters of e-mail were the Zoomers (a paper culture) and e-mail actually increased paper use for many. For Gen X and Gen Y using instant messaging and web-based document storage is second nature.

Eco-friendliness is not a fad. It is a long-term concern for all generations and companies who are willing to go greener with their offices will find they are much more attractive places to work for all of the generations.

57: Customer Service

This is an interesting topic as it relates to business and the generations. Businesses today know that customer service is the key differentiator in creating customer loyalty. The challenge for many companies is that they feel that Gen Y does not have the same "service attitude" that the Zoomers have had to learn and that Gen X has had to adopt. I have a consulting client in the staffing industry and they have a rule that they will only hire "nice" people regardless of the generation they are in. When I talked to the co-owner (it is a husband and wife team) about this, she said that in her fifteen years of experience in the industry people who weren't inherently "nice" did not do well in staffing sales.

When I asked her to clarify "nice" for me she said that she looks for a natural friendliness, an air of approachability, a confident yet humble attitude and a drive to achieve sales. It has worked very well for the company to hire "nice" and you can definitely feel that this is the culture in which they work. People who do get hired and aren't nice do not last very long in the company.

You would have to agree that regardless of age being nice is a key component to providing great customer service. Gen Ys can be perceived as standoffish or have a "you're a pain in the neck" attitude when a customer asks them for something. But in my experience you can be from any generation and still not be great at customer service. It is a skill to learn how to communicate and provide value for a variety of different personalities.

I will never forget when I got promoted from teller to customer service at the bank I would immediately get up to help customers when they came to the side counter. I couldn't believe it when a lady who had been in that department forever chastised me for getting up so quickly. She said, "The customers will expect that all the time." This flabbergasted me even at twenty years of age—it turned out that I have always had a customer service mindset and this lady felt I was making her look bad.

Let's look quickly at the different generational viewpoints on providing customer service.

Zoomers:
- ✓ Customer service is what you do to keep the customer happy and gain more business
- ✓ Customer service is face to face or on the phone
- ✓ Customer service is giving the client exactly what they ask for
- ✓ The customer is always right
- ✓ You can turn a rude customer around
- ✓ You must dress professionally for great first impressions.

Gen X:
- ✓ Customer service helps increase sales
- ✓ Customer service is being quick and responsive
- ✓ Customer service can be provided by e-mail
- ✓ Customers are usually right, but not always
- ✓ You can use humor as a tool to connect with customers
- ✓ You must dress according your day's events; for example, if you have meetings you dress up, otherwise you can be a little more casual.

Gen Y:
- ✓ Customer service is fine when customers are nice to me
- ✓ Customer service does not mean I have to deal with rudeness
- ✓ It's okay if I have tattoos and piercings—everyone has them nowadays
- ✓ Customer service can be provided by instant messaging, a link or an e-mail
- ✓ It's okay if I check my BlackBerry while I wait for you to make up your mind about what you want
- ✓ The customer isn't always right and a rude customer is unacceptable

✓ If a customer doesn't listen to me I will pass it on to my manager so they can deal with it.

As you can see, creating a unified approach from these different attitudes can be a challenge. What I have found is that again if we provide the "big picture" to the Gen Ys (something that may be more than obvious to Gen X and Zoomers) they will buy in to customer service standards. For example, if your company does not allow tattoos or piercings to be visible then you need to go over this with Gen Y hires and provide the bigger-picture reason for the policy. You can also provide support by saying they can put their piercings back in after work, or something similar.

58: SALES

Sales forces are changing rapidly, especially in this new economy in which we no longer really know for sure what the approval channels are or what the current needs might be for the buying client.

It is interesting how Gen Ys look at sales as a natural part of a relationship but selling as a skill is definitely something Gen Ys need to be trained to do.

Zoomers have had years of experience selling in the old economy—you establish a need, you present a product or service, you ask for the order, get the sale and you are done. Many of us, regardless of our generation, found that from about 2004 to 2008 it was fairly easy to get a sale and became "order takers" instead of true sales professionals. When business is robust and money is flowing freely it is easy to get a sale; however, when the economy turns, needs become more specific and purchases need to be justified so it changes the rules for everybody.

Let's look at the general sales attitudes of each of the generations to see how they might view and approach sales in the current economy.

Zoomers have learned sales as a process and as a system of using rapport building techniques, focusing on benefits and then closing the deal. Gen X has learned that being in sales can make them very wealthy and have focused on using technology to help leverage the sales process. Gen Ys see the word "sales" as doing something to someone else so they would much rather focus on building relationships than be told to focus on the "close."

Today Baby Boomers complain about how Generation Ys are shouting out loud about their independence and the fact that they will "change it all" and "like to do things their own way." The fact of the matter is that way back when the Baby Boomers started they were challenging the status quo and finding new ways to communicate and influence the world too—think of fax machines, mobile telephony, the birth of the Internet and twenty-four-hour news channels. Were they any different from today's generation?

Generation Y is the true mobile Internet generation; they live and breathe social media and instant communications. Research shows (from Morgan Stanley's mobile Internet report, 2010) that more than 10 billion mobile Internet devices have been created in the world, compared to 100 million PC units. Up to 830 million people globally use social networking sites and the average time spent on these sites is up by 25 percent in the last year alone. Many believe that sites such as Facebook are fast becoming the main communications platform for the majority in the future—especially for Generation Y.

eMarketer reports that teens today are spending as many as thirteen hours per day online, many of them moving away from the traditional PC on a desk to netbook and smartphone technologies. Mobile Internet usage is three times higher on iPhones than on any other mobile device (Morgan Stanley). Emerging markets are once again skipping a technological generation and moving straight to the mobile Internet as their preferred platform.

So what does this all mean from a sales perspective? Generation Y is the growing sector in the consumer market today; Zoomers are not the future consumer. Face to face sales shows the preference Zoomers have for real conversations with real people. While "face time" may still be needed for the ultimate in issue resolution, the instant gratification generation of Gen Y wants to be able to solve issues quickly and cheaply using the channels they know and understand. If we get it right they are happy and sometimes they tell their friends; if we get it wrong then the whole planet knows five minutes later as the viral messages bloom across the networks. Companies must seriously address sales approach challenges with newer generations. It's not a choice of whether to address it, it's a question of when and how.

59: Operations

In many organizations the typical communication challenge between departments is between Operations and Sales. It is because they have two opposing functions: Sales is supposed to go out and get the business and Operations is supposed to make sure the business can be executed or maintained. In the generational context the perceptions of each of the generations in an operational role can create other challenges. The biggest opportunity for operations departments and sales departments is to help each other see each other's role and understand how their individual roles function.

A consulting client I am working with has service technicians on the road and office staff to handle logistics and operations. I was facilitating a discussion with the operations team about how they could be more efficient as a company and it turned out that the inside operations staff had no idea what the sales and service technicians had to do on a daily basis. We set up a monthly "road trip" for the office staff to go out with sales and service technicians and instantly communication improved. Understanding of the sales and service function increased and, funnily enough, results increased. We then arranged for the sales and service technicians to be in the office for one day to see how operations worked. There was a newfound appreciation for what they went through on a daily basis. By cross-training this way we also received more creative ideas to help solve ongoing problems, found out where individuals were creating process bottlenecks and where skills development was needed.

Let's look at how each generation would generally function in an operations role.

Remembering that Zoomers are structure-oriented and have processes and systems in place that have worked for a very long time, the biggest challenge for Zoomers in operations is to be willing to change the way things have been done. For example, a Zoomer was creating a communication bottleneck at one company because he was reluctant to adopt the use of a BlackBerry to receive e-mail from the office. His reluctance caused major delays in getting back to customers and to operations staff. When we logically laid out why it was necessary for the operations department to reach him and gave him specific examples, he was willing to make the change and adapt to the use of technology for his job.

Gen X has learned structure from the Zoomers but has figured out how to leverage technology and simplify systems put in place by the Zoomers. The challenge with Gen X in an operations capacity is that they "assume" that everyone automatically understands the process and get impatient when they have to revisit procedures or processes with an employee or teammate. One of my consulting clients had two Gen X colleagues, Kris and Viola, in the operations department. Kris was frustrated because Viola was more of an analytical type who wanted responses to her e-mails so she knew they were received. Kris also had a Gen Y report to her who did not see the need to respond to every e-mail sent by Viola. Kris thought that Viola was being petty for pestering her to have the Gen Y respond. When I pointed out to Kris that I thought the Gen Y was purposely not responding to Viola, Kris had to admit that, yes, that was true. So the real issue was one of disrespect and not following protocol! Kris had a conversation with her Gen Y report and asked her to respond to all e-mails to indicate they had been received.

It gets tricky for a Gen Y in an operations function. Unless they are fully trained, given full exposure and are given the full parameters of their role they will often struggle with their identity within the operations department. Companies often say that they want a new hire up and running very quickly and what that usually means is they want to train them in the basics and then let them do their thing. This quickly leads to frustration for the person who hired the Gen Y but is equally frustrating for Gen Ys who do not feel they received full training to do their job in the best way possible. Gen Y also sees areas where technology could simplify processes and they get very frustrated when they are told that their ideas are good but not ready to be implemented.

60: Accounting

Every organization has "departmental personalities" in addition to the individual personalities of those who work in the department. Sales departments often have a Dancer personality—it's the socializing, cool department that gets all of the attention and seems to be having the most fun. The operations department is the Driver personality focused on getting things done quickly and efficiently, the HR department would be the Deflector and the accounting department would be the Detailer in the group.

Remember in the chapter on personalities I said that the Detailer personality is analytical: cross the t's and dot the i's and make sure you have the facts. It would be safe to say that a lot of the employees attracted to an accounting department would have some element of Detailer as one of their primary personality types.

So whether we have a Zoomer, Gen X or Gen Y working in the accounting department they would all likely have the Detailer personality in common. Having said that, even accounting departments are feeling the effects of differing generational viewpoints. I have a client who is the CFO of a major gaming company; she heads up the accounting and finance division. The people in her department are highly educated and highly intelligent in their area of expertise. Where there is a need for individual development is in the area of people (interpersonal) skills. Recently I worked with the accounting department to provide communication skills, helping them interact with different personalities as well as providing conflict management and negotiation skills.

It was interesting to me that the Gen Xs in the department were quite abrupt and straightforward and felt that the other departments didn't appreciate the level of detail required by the accounting department. The Zoomers were a little more relaxed but had an attitude of "we have always done it this way," which the Gen Xs were constantly challenging. The Gen Ys in this particular company were actually quite quiet and low key about their opinions, which is unlike most Gen Ys in general. I realized that in this corporate culture tenure held the power so it quieted the voices of the Gen Ys. When I mentioned this to the CFO she immediately realized that they needed to create a forum for the Gen Ys to speak and contribute their ideas, otherwise the company would move forward with the status quo without gaining the advantage of Gen Y's ideas and input.

I feel that accounting departments are the most undervalued and underappreciated department of most organizations when in fact nobody gets paid without accounting. I make a huge effort to build equal recognition within companies so that people appreciate the work of all of the departments and all of the people within each department.

61: Hiring

Zoomers are facing their successors during the hiring process and cannot begin to fathom that these kids will be half as capable as they are.

Gen X and Y have been taught interview skills in high school, college and university and they are taught how to put a positive spin on anything. In short, they have become professional interviewees. That is why a Zoomer or Gen X manager can interview a Gen Y and ask them how they are on the phone—the Gen Y will say, "Great!" A few days later the manager is cringing as he hears their phone manner.

When hiring Gen Y you need to be very specific. You need to use a situational interview style (where you put them in a typical workplace situation and get them to "try it out" in the interview). This may seem intimidating, but you will soon learn the prospective hire's true skill level by asking them to do a role play with you based on a common customer-facing scenario that the job would require.

Gen Y is also looking for opportunities where they can grow their skill set without sacrificing other areas of their life. As a matter of fact, many Xs and Ys may choose not to take a lucrative or promising position if they see major sacrifice and lack of support, tools or technology. These generations are clear in thinking that the reward or benefit of accepting a position must outweigh any perceived imbalance or cost. To that end, Gen X and Y do not subscribe to the same kind of corporate loyalty that Zoomers had in the past. Gen Y especially is loyal to lifestyle and friends, not work and corporate identity.

When hiring you will want to look strategically at the following:
✓ What is the position and what education and skill set is required?

- ✓ Which generation is best suited to the position, given what we know to be true about each of the generations?
- ✓ What is the career path for the position or within the company and what can we promise in three months? Six months? A year? Beyond a year?
- ✓ What are the expectations regarding start time, breaks and finish time within the company culture?
- ✓ What other industries might have people who would be well suited for this position?
- ✓ Who did we hire that was a good fit for a similar position and do they know others who could be as well?
- ✓ What type of referral fee are we willing to pay to find good people?
- ✓ Do we offer hiring incentives, and if so, what are they?
- ✓ What is the full job description?
- ✓ Who will they report to? What is the personality of the person they will report to? What is the interviewee's personality?
- ✓ What are the success checkpoints once they are hired to make sure they are on track for their ninety-day probationary period job review and job satisfaction check-in?

When hiring with the generations in mind we want to think about the motivators for each of the generations as well as how we can set them up to succeed quickly within the organization.

62: Discipline

"Do it or you're fired!"

Sound familiar? If it does, you are likely a Zoomer. There is no way that kind of threat would hold any water with a Gen Y. A Gen X would pay attention to some extent because they generally have a mortgage so the money is important, but good portions of Gen Ys are still living at home. Many don't leave until the age of thirty-five (yes, you saw that right). Even if your Gen Y has left home statistics say they are coming back at least once before they leave permanently, and that makes them less apt to worry about being fired. When Zoomers left home (typically at eighteen) they didn't want to ever go back. The threat of "do it or you're fired" held the possibility of being forced to go home so they did what was needed to keep their jobs.

Employee discipline is an HR function but I believe there are distinct ways to talk to each of the generations so that they hear you and respond the way you want them to. I don't really like the word "discipline" because it implies harshness, but it is a necessary term in regards to workplace rules.

In my experience companies with the fewest rules tend to have the least need to discipline their employees. Larger organizations, of course, have more complex structures, systems and rules and therefore need to have some form of keeping things in order, which is really what discipline is.

I also feel that discipline becomes unnecessary or minimally necessary if the guidelines for behavior and expectations for performance are clearly communicated and even rewarded. For example, instead of penalizing employees for being late some companies reward those employees who are consistently on time. It's like replacing negative motivation (discipline) with positive motivation (reward for the behavior you wanted in the first place).

The keys to successful discipline are:

✓ Ensure you state what the expectations are at the point of hire

✓ Catch them doing what you want and recognize and reward in the short term (for example, comment on their promptness in the first week of hire)

✓ If they deviate from the rules or expectations, have a one-on-one conversation and ask open-ended questions such as, "Was there a reason why you were late this morning?"

✓ Re-state the expectations.

If they continue the unacceptable behavior you then have to advise them that you will be documenting the conversation, outline specific actions you would like them to take and state the consequences if they do not. Provide a timeframe for them to meet your requests and check in regularly.

Zoomers are familiar with disciplinary action due to their length of time in the workplace, while Gen X responds to a positive approach and Gen Y needs to be held accountable to acceptable behavior and then rewarded when they do it right.

63: Conflict Management

When you have different personalities, work styles and generations you will inevitably end up with conflict situations. The basics of conflict management still apply when dealing with intergenerational conflict. Let's look at the concepts of conflict management before bringing in the ways to prevent it in the first place.

Conflict management is all about creating awareness and perspective around what someone wants and why they want it. Once we understand these two things we can find our way to bridging the conflict barrier and coming to a new understanding.

Many of us in all generations avoid conflict because it is uncomfortable, awkward or embarrassing. The truth is that conflict is an opportunity for growth. Typically after any conflict we can acknowledge that something has to change, and often it is our own perspective that needs changing!

The differences in values and opinions between the generations tend to increase conflict. Let's take a look at varying viewpoints on certain elements of work with each of the generations and see how the viewpoints could lead to conflict.

Generation	Zoomer	Gen X	Gen Y
Workplace	Structure	Balance	Fun
Tasks	Checklist	Outlook	BlackBerry
Marriage	Long term	Kids	Why?
Time off	Relax	Family	Adventure
Parents	Aging	Babysitters	Still at home
Quitting time	When work done	By dinner	By the clock

You can see from just the few examples above the variance in viewpoints and each of the items can lead to conflict.

The key to resolving conflict is to use universal communication that respects and honors the position of the other person. In every conflict there is the person's "interest" and their "position." The interest is what they want and the position is why they want it. For example, if two little girls both want an orange and there is only one orange, the obvious solution would be to cut the orange in half. However, if we used conflict resolution skills we would want to find out first what they both want (the orange), and then we would want to find out why they want it, which is where the creative solution would arise. So if little girl #1 wants to eat the orange and little girl #2 wants the orange peel to make potpourri then we could definitely make sure both girls could get what they want and end the conflict.

With the generations we want to look beneath the surface issue to find out what is really going on. Using a work example, let's assume a Zoomer wants holidays at the same time as their Gen Y counterpart and yet only one of them can get that vacation time. We want to find out why the Zoomer wants those holidays. Let's say it's just to take a week off to relax. Then we ask why the Gen Y wants holidays and we find out it's to go to a family reunion celebrating his grandma's ninetieth birthday. Based on that information the Zoomer would likely be willing to take the week before or after. However, if the Zoomer feels he or she is "entitled" to that specific time based on tenure then they might force the issue unnecessarily in my opinion and create a greater conflict.

You can see how generational attitudes can create more tension and more conflict if individuals are unwilling to take personal responsibility for their positions and interests.

64: WORK EXPERIENCE

In Chapter Eight we talked about workers' experiences at work. In this chapter we look at the different levels of work experience that each generation brings to the table.

In Chapter Forty Nine we talked about the different levels of education each of the generations has as well as the different ways they look at education. Let's look at work experience from a generational standpoint to see where some of the conflicts in work styles can come up.

Here's a quick look at work education again very quickly.

	Zoomer	Gen X	Gen Y
High School	Yes	Yes	Yes
College	Some	Yes	Yes
University	Some	Some	Yes
Degrees	Some	Some	Yes

Many Zoomers have gained and are gaining further education later in life. Many Gen Xers are getting their degrees while working and many Gen Ys are coming in to the workplace with some amount of university education. The reason for this is that Zoomer parents are insisting that their children go to university to get a good job. The parents of many Zoomers couldn't afford university, so they were forced to go out and work. This is how we end up with differing viewpoints on work experience.

Based on age alone it stands to reason that Zoomers have the most job experience of all three generations. Often this is a bone of contention for both employers and the Zoomers themselves, who believe that without experience in the workplace who is going to know what to do when the Zoomers retire?

The work experience of the Gen X is based less on tenure; however, they have had to become more efficient than their Zoomer counterparts because they are less inclined to want to stay late. The challenge for Gen X is getting the Zoomer to share knowledge and work experience. What the Gen X may lack in on-the-job experience they could gain from effective teaching and sharing by Zoomers.

The Gen Ys are in the classic Catch-22. They do not have the work experience but they do have the education. To gain the work experience they need the opportunity to get the job, get the training and to prove themselves.

Earlier I talked about job sharing within organizations. I believe this will solve the work experience dilemma for the Gen Ys as they will be able to cite experience with a company within a pool of shared talent, which will help them transfer those skills to a new job. The important aspect of this topic is that the Zoomers are willing to download what they know to Gen X and Gen Y, and Gen X is willing to transfer what they know to the Gen Y as well. What the Gen Ys lack in work experience they more than make up for in education and technical knowledge.

65: HEALTH

Each of the generations has its own unique health challenges. The leading health issues among Zoomers can be categorized as partially resulting from lifestyle habits indulged in by this age group more than any other. These habits include for some, smoking, inadequate diet and poor exercise. The most common conditions experienced by Zoomers today are: heart disease; kidney disease; arterial sclerosis; osteoporosis; breast, lung, and colon cancer; stroke; and joint complaints such as bursitis, arthritis and tendonitis, just to name a few!

Although Gen Xs took their time to develop careers, married late and postponed having children, they are now buying homes and having children at a higher rate than in the previous decade. As of the year 1998, the birth rate had increased 2 percent, the first increase in birth rates in seven years. By the year 2000, close to two-thirds, or 65 percent, of women ages twenty-five to thirty-four had had children.

Smoking-related health issues also may begin to climb as Gen X ages, since smoking rates for people twenty-five to forty-four years old were highest at 25.6 percent, as reported by the Centers for Disease Control and Prevention in 2003. The smoking rate for men in this age group is 28.4 percent; for women it's 22.8 percent. Other health issues include depression, anxiety and eating disorders.

Depression and anxiety are issues for many of this generation due to the many stressors related to their upbringing and social expectations. Parental divorce rates, which climbed quickly during their developmental years and on into young adulthood, have contributed to the incidence of depression among this group. Yet delayed treatment for depression is not uncommon because divorce is often viewed as normal and Gen

X fears being viewed as weak and less competitive in the marketplace. Confusion and anxiety related to developing meaningful intimacy are also issues for this generation.

Eating disorders also affect this generation. Extreme thinness—now associated with success, achievement and class—is considered a plus, is reinforced by men of this generation and is associated with a woman's ability to contribute to the financial stability of the family.

When it comes to health and wellness, Gen Y is less concerned about most things than the rest of the population—no surprise. However, where a marked and concerning difference emerges is in their levels of stress and fatigue. According to the Health Focus Trend Study, their key health concerns do not mirror those of the general population. Their top five concerns (in order) are tiredness, stress, cancer, depression and cardiovascular disease. Twenty-eight percent of eighteen to twenty-nine-year-olds report being affected by depression. This is five percentage points higher than the general population, a significant difference.

Gen Y is actually an upbeat generation secure in its self worth and ability to succeed. But according to *USA Today*, the trauma with which this group has grown up is shaping their outlook to a large degree. This is a group that has grown up not only with foreign wars but with repeated domestic tragedies—9/11, Hurricane Katrina, Columbine, and recently the Haiti earthquake.

In addition their childhood, filled with planned activities, has extended into their adult lives so they are very busy and overtaxed. Twenty-eight percent describe their diets as unhealthy versus only 19 percent of the total population; almost half of them wish they had time to exercise more versus a third of the total population; and 29 percent say they smoke compared to 19 percent of the total population.

Organizations that provide health and wellness to each of the generations in the form of exercise benefits, reward and recognition programs for keeping staff fit and other illness prevention programs will hold more appeal in the near future for all of the generations.

66: Department Silos

Departments within organizations can often become separated or an entity of their own within the organization. We call these "departmental silos."

A study by *Industry Week* found that business functions operating as silos are the biggest hindrance to corporate growth. A more recent American Management Association survey shows that 83 percent of executives said that silos existed in their companies and that 97 percent think they have a negative effect.

In a recent *Wall Street Journal* article on the latest business buzzwords, the word "un-siloing" was listed.

Power struggles happen everywhere–in any industry. Silos can be created around an individual or a group such as a generation, a division, a function or even a product line. Wherever it's found, silo mentality becomes synonymous with power struggles, lack of cooperation, and loss of productivity. Silos can destroy an enterprise: The organization fragments into a group of camps that have little incentive to collaborate, share information or team up to pursue project goals. Local leaders focus on serving their individual agendas—often at the expense of the rest of the organization. The resulting internal battles over authority, finances and resources destroy productivity and jeopardize the achievement of corporate objectives. Talented (and frustrated) employees walk out the door—or worse yet, stay and become apathetic.

What can be done to tear down silos, reduce conflicts and increase collaboration in a multigenerational workplace? Here are a few ideas:

Reward teamwork: Include collaboration as a critical skill on performance reviews and recognize employees who collaborate successfully with each other, other departments and other generations.

Value Innovation: Innovation happens when ideas are met with an open attitude and a desire to integrate new ideas into systems. Creativity and ideas shared among teams are what is going to drive businesses forward.

Open Communication: When departments share information and information is freely relayed from the top down silos are broken down. It is when information is hoarded or lorded over another person or department that the silo mentality takes firm hold. Where suitable, use communication tools like instant messaging, video updates from departments and internal news outlets to keep the whole company informed of what each department is doing.

Build Trust: Relationships thrive in an environment of personal trust. Trust grows out of experience and interaction—usually extended over time by talking and asking questions, by listening and seeing actions match words. But it is also built by getting to know people as individuals. When you hold offsite retreats, organization-wide celebrations, or workplace events with "social" time built in, you provide opportunities for employees to develop camaraderie and personal relationships of trust.

67: EMPLOYEE ENGAGEMENT

Older workers are more likely to have higher levels of workplace engagement than younger workers, according to a new study by the Sloan Center on Aging and Work at Boston College.

This is important because "engagement"—defined as "a positive, fulfilling work-related state of mind that is characterized by vigor, dedication and absorption," is an important factor that contributes to workplace productivity and innovation, according to the study "Engaging the 21st Century Multi-Generational Workforce."

Happily for all, the methods to increase employee engagement are similar for all ages and generations. The study finds that employees of all ages and generations are more likely to have higher engagement at work when they:

✓ Are satisfied with the training and development opportunities available to them;

✓ Are working in teams that have a culture supportive of workplace flexibility; and

✓ Receive investments from employers in their benefits programs, especially health insurance for family members of full-time employees, life insurance and employer contributions to defined contribution plans.

High levels of employee engagement are especially important in the current economic crisis. Engaged employees are generally more productive and innovative—key factors to surviving in this economy. Additionally, studies show that engaged employees use less health care, take fewer sick days, have longer tenure and create stronger customer relationships.

The survey of approximately 2200 employees across the country on various factors of employee engagement disputes commonly held assumptions that engagement is a "condition of youthful energy," as aging has long been considered as a time for disengagement due to time on the job, readiness to retire or a developed cynicism. Rather engagement isn't about age or generation, it is about emotional engagement with the organization, the people they work with and the customers they serve.

68: Performance Reviews

Do you regularly hear the following from a Gen Y: "Hey boss, how am I doing?" If you have heard this then you are experiencing the Gen Y's keen desire to be given ongoing guidance. They also usually want to hear the good stuff and seem to get instantly demotivated if the feedback isn't given in an upbeat and future-focused delivery style.

Having a strategic, focused review system is more important now than ever before. Clear performance goals provide better business results and a greater employee return on investment. With at least three generations of employees in your workforce, you need to be able to understand and address the needs of all your employees.

While a recent college graduate may appreciate 360° feedback, that process may be baffling and uncomfortable to an employee approaching retirement. Personalized reviews improve relevance. Making sure that your review system is up to date and can provide multiple raters that include peers, clients and your leaders may be critical to your success.

As a consultant I have worked with a number of companies that have no formalized performance reviews. Usually they are companies with revenues of less than $5 million a year and while they have grown aggressively they have not put performance measurement and review systems in place. Recently I helped clients determine the best performance review process for their small company. We determined that a short two-page review was best because the majority of their employees were Gen Ys looking for more ongoing and frequent performance reviews versus using a four or five-page annual performance review format.

I actually dislike annual reviews if they are done without ongoing feedback for the employees. Many Zoomers view the performance review with a degree of cynicism because they may have experienced the Traditionalists' delivery style, which was critical and punitive so it wasn't a motivational tool. I believe this is why it is difficult for Zoomers to give ongoing praise to Gen Y—because they themselves did not receive it in the workplace.

Gen X is truly appreciative of the performance review process. They see it as an opportunity to point out training needs and career path focus. A good performance review provides excellent positive reinforcement coupled with practical ideas for improvement. Specific examples of project completion, customer results or sales growth should be included so that you are recognizing the behaviors that you want the employee to continue. Where improvement is needed it is important for leaders to provide resources and tools to help the Gen X or Gen Y employee to improve his or her performance. Today many companies are connecting job performance to pay and/or profit sharing, which is very appealing to all of the generations.

WestJet, a Canadian airline, is a great example of an organization that has built loyal Gen X and Y employees by calling every employee a "partner" as well as building their performance reviews around customer care and teamwork.

A question to ask yourself is, "Do I conduct my performance reviews with the generational viewpoints taken into account, and how can I improve my feedback and performance review process?"

69: 360 DEGREE REVIEWS

A 360-degree performance appraisal system is a multisource assessment approach that taps the collective wisdom of those who work closely with an employee. The employee and their supervisors, colleagues, direct reports (subordinates), internal customers, external customers and others may be part of the evaluation process.

Proponents of the 360-degree feedback approach offer it as a "progressive" means of conducting performance appraisals. Many would argue that 360-degree feedback systems and other forms of multisource or multirater assessment methods have evolved from an innovative "nice-to-have" technique administered only to the most senior levels to a "must-have" tool for integration into overall performance and human resource management strategies. These systems appear well suited to the multi-generational, team-based, change-oriented organizational cultures of many organizations today.

360-degree systems are gaining in popularity because they tend to reduce the problems of previous generations of assessment methods. A 360-degree appraisal moves managers (as appraisers) back into the "comfort zone" as they are now only one among a number of assessors. It greatly reduces the problems of subjective reviews by one person, such as favouritism or biases in ratings that plague the traditional boss–subordinate approach. A 360-degree appraisal also reduces defensiveness on the part of the person being reviewed because a variety of assessors is involved and feedback is presented as more balanced.

However, to make it work properly organizations must resolve the issue of what is meant by job effectiveness in the context of that particular business and what behaviors are causally related to it. The technique is also helpful in defending legal challenges of appraisal outcomes, meets employee demands for empowerment and involvement and finally, it is a useful tool in tapping into employee opinions and attitudes.

It is an especially useful tool for the multi-generational and multicultural workplace. Recently I facilitated a 360-degree performance review for the leaders of a small company. It was done in a unique format that suited this small company but we had all the leaders complete the ratings and comments for the leader being reviewed. We then delivered the results in a facilitated meeting and it was extremely powerful.

There are a variety of ways to conduct 360 reviews. In the example I provided we simply had leaders rate their peer leaders. A more in-depth version would result if we went to the employees, customers and suppliers. For instance, subordinates are best placed to assess "leadership" or "people management" skills, while suppliers provide useful feedback on how the leader interacts with them.

The 360-degree review is a great objective tool that allows companies to integrate multiple perceptions from many sources, providing a truly multidimensional performance review that leads to greater improvements in performance.

70: Presentations

As someone who gives presentations to multigenerational audiences I have noticed there are distinct differences among the responses of the generations in an audience.

Good presenters will know who is in their audience and that includes knowing the unique viewpoints of each of the generations. I mentioned earlier that I do not get offended when a Gen Y or Gen X texts from their PDA while in a meeting. Yet I have met many Zoomers who find this behavior disrespectful. This is because a Zoomer has worked in professional environments where you give a presenter your full attention. Because of this they believe that all people in an audience should behave "respectfully."

Because Gen Xs were the early adopters of BlackBerrys they see nothing wrong with quickly responding to an e-mail. They think this is more polite than leaving the meeting and disrupting the presentation.

As I said in previous chapters, Gen Y takes notes on their PDAs and often will tweet or IM a colleague to give instant feedback on the content of the presentation.

I think it's important when giving presentations to set behavior expectations before the meeting even starts. You might say, "Please turn off all PDAs," or "Please put your PDAs on silent."

When you are presenting please keep the following in mind about how each of the generations learn and want to receive information.

Zoomers: They like practical, relevant and useable data. They like stories that they can relate to, such as the work environment and how it has changed over the years. They are okay with you using a flip chart or a whiteboard.

Gen X: They like fast paced presentations. Do not read slides and insult their intelligence. Allow them to interact with your presentation using text messaging or e-mail during the event. Give them permission to tweet elements of your presentation. They like slides, but keep them clean with little text and lots of graphics or pictures.

Gen Y: Use humor, fun activities and interaction to make the learning fun. Use graphics, animation and videos. Gen Y loves to participate, so audience participation is a good bet with this age group.

71: Ethics

Several managers have said to me that they are concerned about Gen Y's ethics and have doubts about their integrity. Many other managers have said they have trouble trusting their young employees.

Many Gen Ys would find this offensive, but I can also understand where the managers are coming from. For example, I know many young adults (including my stepsons) who buy or are given a video game and immediately go online to get the cheat codes to beat the game. Is that ethical? I also know a few young ladies who buy a nice dress to wear to a party and then return it the day after the celebration. Is that ethical?

Is Gen Y really lacking in ethics? Or do they simply prefer shortcuts? Or does every generation have challenges with ethics?

Ethics have never been more important to the careers of all of the generations. Headlines about companies that have imploded due to lack of ethics continue to hit the news. At the same time, getting a reputation for being unethical can leave a lasting stain on an otherwise impressive résumé. Doing the right thing may not always be the easiest path, but it is the path that keeps you looking forward instead of over your shoulder.

Some basic ethics for each individual in the workplace are:

Résumés: Lying on or embellishing résumés has reached epidemic proportions. You can point out positive elements but do not lie about your education or your work experience.

Confidentiality: Keeping your work confidential is part of being a professional.

Theft: You don't have to pocket cash from your employer for it to be considered stealing.

Silence: If you see someone stealing or bypassing protocols and systems you must speak up. Silence is corroboration.

You need to be able to bring up anything that doesn't feel right with the boss or HR without fear of repercussions.

72: COACHING

As a management and leadership tool, coaching is becoming an even more valued instrument in the workplace than ever before. In fact many organizations have been outsourcing coaching for their leaders and those who are being groomed for future leadership.

Coaching requires a fair amount of focused time and follow-up. In my experience, the only reason coaching does not get the attention it deserves is because of the time involved.

Companies recognize the importance of coaching and they also recognize that phenomenal coaching requires a focused and systematic approach to helping the person being coached to succeed.

Unlike training or mentoring, business coaching is a combination of personal coaching and helping the person transfer their personal skills to the job environment. A skilled coach looks for unique motivators specific to the person they are coaching and then works to connect their personal attributes with the skills needed for high performance in their role.

Many leaders have heard the term "coaching" and they think they are providing it for their teams, but in reality it is more than that. It is about holding the person being coached to a systematic skill development, accountability and follow-up program.

In my experience here is how each of the generations prefers to be coached:

Zoomers: They have a great deal of accomplishment and skill development already. They want their experience to be acknowledged. The best coaching approach for Zoomers is a peer assessment format, in which they can see irrefutable evidence of what areas they could improve. Once armed with this information I find Zoomers are eager to improve their skills.

Gen X: The Gen Xs that I have coached (and still coach) are direct, abrupt and have large egos. They have had to fight to get where they are so they tend to have a high level of bravado. I have noticed that they look for coaching on how to be more assertive instead of aggressive and they want to find ways to get promotions and recognition.

Gen Y: The Gen Ys I coach love the one-on-one attention of having a coach. They are eager to learn all the insider tricks and tips that will help them succeed with the Zoomers and Gen Xs. They benefit from advice on how to approach their older peers with research, preparation and professionalism.

73: Sabbaticals

Sabbaticals originated in academia. Most colleges and universities awarded them to professors every seven years as a time for rest and reflection, as if that milestone year were a kind of Sabbath. Intel maintains this traditional schedule. Under a program that began in 1981, the Santa Clara, CA chipmaker grants all full-timers a paid eight-week holiday on every anniversary divisible by seven, along with their usual three to four weeks of vacation. Stitch the time together with a few paid holidays and it's possible to be away without interruption for a quarter of the year. Some 4350 workers, or nearly one of every twenty at Intel, take sabbaticals in a given year.

These days many companies view employees as a drain on profits, particularly stagnant long timers who have received pay raises year after year. Across the economy, a small group of employers are treating workers like tenured professors, providing paid sabbaticals for them. Leaders insist that providing sabbaticals actually helps the bottom line. Giving employees a periodic long break is a welcome change from the world of networked, always-on careers that lead to information overload. Sabbaticals can help reduce turnover and retain the hardworking workers otherwise lost when Zoomer employees burn out. A recent study in the *Journal of Education for Business* found that the benefits of sabbaticals outweigh the costs when a good understanding exists between employer and employee regarding what is to be involved. The study also found that employees return more engaged and re-energized.

In fact, sabbaticals are so alluring that companies report that it's almost impossible for competitors to lure anyone to leave their employer within a few years of a bonus vacation. Sabbaticals also give managers a chance to see how well others perform while filling in for their on-leave colleagues.

The number of companies offering paid sabbaticals is steadily growing. An annual survey by the Society for Human Resource Management finds that 5 percent of corporate respondents offer the perk. Another 18 percent offer unpaid sabbaticals, which are increasingly being used as an alternative to layoffs when demand slackens.

On the other hand, relative newcomers such as women's clothing designer Eileen Fisher Inc. have initiated sabbaticals, while McDonald's Corp., where the perk dates back more than forty years, expanded the benefit in 2006 to once every five years. "What it's all about today is, how do you differentiate yourself as a company?" says Richard Floersch, McDonald's chief human resources officer. "This gives us bragging rights."

Some would ask, "Won't regular old vacations do"? Studies have found they don't allow enough time for rest and reflection. A third of employees don't even take all of their time off, with the same number reporting that they feel chronically overstressed at work, according to a recent study by the Families & Work Institute.

The biggest reason more companies don't offer sabbaticals, of course, is money. A company has to overstaff to be able to allow employees more time off, and that's often heresy at a time when management is scrounging for ways to slash personnel expenses. Scheduling can be a headache, too, since managers have to find others to cover for every worker away on leave.

But many HR managers argue that since sabbaticals encourage people to stick around, companies don't have to spend as much on recruitment and training. Assigning temporary fill-ins can be a plus, too. While Intel's Melanie Stagnitti, a compensation and benefits manager, was on sabbatical, her supervisor tested someone else in her job. When she came back that employee ended up staying on and Stagnitti was promoted to a new job in HR. In addition, the generation just entering the workforce ranks time off as a top priority in survey after survey. Thus, offering sabbaticals should help attract young talent, says Hewitt consultant Raymond Baumruk.

Probably no company has handed out more sabbaticals than McDonald's. Like employees elsewhere, McDonald's loyalists often use their sabbaticals for blowout vacations. Not Janice L. Fields. The president of McDonald's central US division, Fields travels three or four days every week to oversee 4400 outlets. She spent her eight-week leave last winter with her retired husband, Doug Wilkens, at their second home in Florida.

She slept in. She worked out. She played golf. She cooked. She watched *Oprah*. She reconnected with her spouse. And she left town only once, to go to Cincinnati for her grandson's eighth birthday. After twenty-seven years at Big Mac, she deserved a break. And thanks to the company's sabbatical program, she got one.

74: PARENTAL LEAVE

In the benefits chapter I mentioned that all of the generations are looking for customized benefit options that suit their unique and individual lifestyles. Many companies have recognized that parental leave is unique to each situation.

According to a study by The Economic Policy Institute, the United States ranks lowest in terms of maternity leave. The study performed in May, 2009 compares seven countries, including the US. The following list shows how these countries rank in maternity leave benefits:

United Kingdom: Provides a total of fifty-two weeks of maternity leave, which includes fifteen weeks of paid leave.

Italy: Provides a total of twenty weeks of maternity leave, which includes fifteen weeks of paid leave.

France: Provides a total of fifteen weeks of maternity leave, all paid.

Canada: Provides a total of fourteen weeks of maternity leave, which includes ten weeks of paid leave.

Germany: Provides fifteen weeks of maternity leave, all paid.

Japan: Provides twelve weeks of maternity leave, which includes ten weeks of paid leave.

United States: Provides twelve weeks of maternity leave for employers with fifty or more employees. All twelve weeks are unpaid unless the employer has a disability benefit program.

I believe the US has lagged behind because many Zoomers didn't push for this as a benefit. Gen X and Gen Ys are looking at parental leave plans as part of their job search. We will see US companies shore up paid parental leave in their efforts to attract and retain Gen X and Gen Y.

I mentioned earlier that alternative family arrangements are also changing the way companies offer parental leave. Progressive companies have plans in place for couples opting for *in vitro* programs, same-sex couples who adopt and individuals choosing to be single parents.

We have come a long way from the days where our family life suffered for our professional efforts. Gen X and Gen Y truly do believe they can have it all and are looking to employers to provide them with options.

Some other important information on how America ranks on a variety of issues is available at this site: http://rankingamerica.wordpress. com/how-does-the-united-states-rank-in/ .

75: Expectations

The biggest challenge I see in organizations is communication breakdown. When communication stagnates or does not remain a high priority people will make up stories about what is going on and then morale can plummet quickly.

A big part of communication is communicating expectations. Many leaders I coach claim frustration when dealing with challenging employees and I always ask if they had clearly outlined their expectations for these workers. Typically the leader will say, "Yes, I have told them over and over again." Then I go on to ask if they have set expectations with a big-picture overview and what the consequences are if the expectations are not met. Typically I get a sheepish look from the leader and they say, "Well, no."

Gen Y specifically needs to know what is expected, why it is expected and what will happen if the expectations aren't met. Zoomers and Gen X need expectations as well, but it seems to me that managers have more frustrations around the Gen Ys "not getting it" or "not having common sense." This points out the need for Zoomer and Gen X leaders to become very clear in setting expectations.

The important part of expectations is understanding what each of the generations expects in general. The leader then must work to match their work expectations with the individual in a way that there is clear understanding and agreement.

I can think of a great example from a TV show called *LA Ink*. It's a show about Kat VonD, a tattoo artist, and her shop. Most Gen Ys would know about this show. On a recent episode Kat hired a Gen Y as a shop manager but didn't tell her that there is more than one shop manager.

The Gen Y expected that with the title of Shop Manager she would be in charge of everyone. When she found out that the actual head manager was a Zoomer she was upset and began to use passive-aggressive behavior to get more recognition and to diminish the credibility of the Zoomer. If Kat had let the Gen Y know upon hiring her that she runs a team shop environment, that every shop manager is responsible for specific duties and that there was a Zoomer as the head shop manager the Gen Y would have known from the outset what to expect.

I often see leaders who do not take the time to communicate expectations around culture. They assume that people will have common sense about the workplace cultural behaviors that have become established within the company. For example, explaining that the culture expects all staff to participate in after-hours social events would be important to explain given that a Gen Y might want to leave early. You know what happens when we "assume."

76: FUN

A Zoomer might read this chapter and think, "What's fun got to do with it?" The Zoomer culture has come from such a hard work mindset that they see fun in the workplace as a waste of time. Gen X and Gen Y are looking for levity in the workplace—they believe you can have fun and get lots done.

Studies have shown that companies that have fun at work have higher levels of productivity, morale and loyalty. Fun expert Jody Urquhart has these thirteen tips for fun in the workplace:

THIRTEEN STEPS TO CREATING A FUN WORKPLACE

1. Give up the notion that professionalism means being serious all the time. It's possible to take yourself lightly and still be competent and productive. Promote the benefits of humor at work.

2. Define what fun is in your workplace and what it is not (e.g. harmful humor, off-color jokes, sexual humor, humor tarnishing the organization).

3. Organize a "Fun Committee" for dreaming up fun stuff to do during and after work.

4. Add fun to meetings. Bring in fun things such as nerf balls, a basketball and hoop, or party blowers. Start a meeting with a humorous story or joke.

5. Collect and share your favorite cartoons and jokes. Create a Joke Board or a Humor Newsletter. Look for ways to disseminate fun and funny things daily.

6. Let customers know you are a fun company. Do something just for fun (organize fun customer events, dress for fun,

share funny things with customers) and give employees tools to create a fun relationship with customers (stickers, candy for children, dog biscuits for dogs, humorous buttons with the company logo). This makes work more fun for employees and it strengthens relationships with customers. Dick Snow of Ben and Jerry's Ice Cream says, "We believe that we're in the entertainment business and selling ice cream is just a part of what we do. In our stores the counter is our stage and the customers are our audience." Disneyland has the same kind of approach. Employees are part of an entertainment experience, and they aren't just doing a job.

7. Gather your co-workers for a "Joy of Work" hour. Everyone must talk about something good at work. Take turns telling stories about the things that make work a joy. Each person should contribute ideas on how to make work more fun.

8. Have a fun recognition program. Fun is not a reward for performance but can be a way to encourage employees to perform. For example, you could create games out of productive activity, like who can motivate the most patients in a hospital to smile or say something funny to the head nurse. Playful and goal-oriented fun is best.

9. Respond to fun when it happens. Funny things occur all the time, but if you are obsessed with left-brain analytical thought, you might find it hard to stop and respond. Natural spontaneous humor is a blessing. Take a moment to give employees and customers an opportunity to see the fun in an event.

10. Commit to being fun and it will change your approach to work. Start slowly with a few activities and communicate your desire to create a more relaxed workplace. Don't expect things to turn around overnight.

11. Put fun things and activities in the staff room. This allows people to take their mind off of the seriousness of work for a short period, so they come back to work with a more positive and balanced perspective.

12. Encourage staff to leave work behind at the end of the day. Employees shouldn't be so consumed with work that it affects their family life and leisure activities. Find fun ways

for employees to "unload" at the end of the day or week. Create a ritual like writing a "to do" list and posting it on the board. By doing this you commit to not thinking about the things on the list until the next day.

13. Encourage employees to develop their own styles of having fun. A nurse anesthetist at a hospital in Michigan often sings to his patients to help them relax prior to surgery. Patients have appreciated this so much that they have told family and friends about the experience. It is not uncommon now for the hospital staff to get requests for "the singing anesthesiologist" when they are scheduling surgeries.

77: ENTERTAINMENT

We are such a culture of reality TV, media and blockbuster movies that many Gen Y respond very well to the notion of entertainment in the workplace. I spoke for Auto Owners Insurance in Lansing, MI last year. They put on annual events for their customers where they bring in an outside expert. They also do fabulous door prize draws for the attendees and they have Gen Y team members who portray funny characters. The customers of Auto Owners are invited to the event at no expense to themselves other than their travel, and the annual event is a huge hit as you can well imagine. The event is successful because of the entertainment factor. Interestingly enough, the Gen Y employees love doing the event and morale is extremely high following it.

As a Gen X–Zoomer cusp baby, I love to be entertained and as a speaker I try to be entertaining with my audiences. At this particular event with Auto Owners my entertainment skills were tested. Their planned entertainer didn't work out for them so literally within forty-eight hours they put together a karaoke show complete with characters, costumes and fun.

They asked me if I would sing karaoke as part of the entertainment. At first I wanted to say no because I really can't sing that well anymore (I used to be able to) and I didn't want to embarrass myself. But then I remembered that people love it when their leaders or guest speakers make fools of themselves. So I sang a really poor version of "These Boots Are Made for Walking" and the audience roared. I thought I did a terrible job but I was a good sport about it. Well, apparently they enjoyed me making a fool of myself so much that they asked me to sing a follow-up duet with their president and we sang a pretty fair version of "Bridge Over Troubled Water."

The point is that entertainment, whether the employees are providing it or it is being provided, can do a lot to keep employees engaged.

A financial client of mine recently had a meeting at which they set up a version of Wii bowling for their whole team during the lunch breaks. This simple idea created Wii bowling challenges and lots of fun on breaks.

So, in my opinion, "let us entertain them!"

78: Reverse Mentoring

We talked about the need for Zoomers to mentor and coach Gen X and Gen Y but a few progressive companies are recognizing the value of cross-mentoring or reverse-mentoring, which I mentioned briefly in an earlier chapter.

It seems scary to have Gen Y mentor a Zoomer because we're used to an older generation assuming the mentor role in work environments. Traditionally it's the high-seniority professionals showing the younger, less experienced mentees the ropes.

If you're of the Zoomer generation you've probably noticed a reverse mentoring trend happening in the workplace. It's essentially Generation Y mentoring the well-established, more experienced workforce as opposed to the other way around. The trend is most noticeable in professional fields where technology is an integral part of the work.

Zoomers should listen to Gen Ys and watch their habits to gain creative insight into how to improve business practices, customer delivery and technology to ease workloads.

It's Gen Y's time to challenge outdated norms and create real change in a business environment where everyone can win.

More and more companies are formalizing reverse mentoring programs by assigning younger people to act as technology guides. The Edelman public relations firm is a good example of this trend. The agency has named its program Rotnem (mentor spelled backwards) and gone worldwide with it. About 95 percent of the senior executives in its Chicago office are working with assigned Rotnems.

Learning how to do it is only half the game. The rest of the equation—understanding the protocol and learning the appropriate way to employ it so that it benefits the organization—is equally challenging. It takes some doing (and a healthy ego) for senior executives to get comfortable with being taught by a younger person.

"You feel stupid," says Janet Cabot, president of Edelman's central region. "… You get to a certain age and you don't want to feel stupid."

Organizations that have instituted reverse mentoring programs often find that the benefits go beyond improved use of technology. Breaching the hard and fast lines of corporate hierarchies is number one among these. Inevitably younger mentors and their pupils are exposed to each other's knowledge and experience.

While benefiting from informed guidance on how to use technology, seniors are gaining insight into what makes their younger associates tick and how to manage them.

"Even though I learned about the networking, what I really learned… it is important to understand what Rotnems think and how they spend their time," says Kathy Krenger, forty-two, an executive at Edelman.

"The mentoring, the sharing (of) diverse perspectives of an older generation versus a younger generation… produces a lot of magic. It breeds innovative thought," declares Raphael Viton, president of an innovation agency in suburban Chicago.

Seniors get a chance to spot and evaluate new talent. At the same time, young people gain exposure to senior executives, which carries with it opportunities to learn from them not only what to do, but also how to get things done.

This exposure includes two other opportunities for young mentors. One, they have a chance to show their capabilities and their work ethic. Second, they can introduce new technologies and strategies that can benefit their employers and by extension themselves.

It's clear. Either way, all parties—employer, senior executives and younger associates—benefit when reverse mentoring takes place.

79: Remote Offices

Working remotely is appealing to all of the generations, but for different reasons.

It's one thing to know how to communicate with people who are in your office but one of the big challenges for many organizations is keeping teams connected and on task when the teams are spread out in various offices.

Technology has come a long way in helping with this. With web sites like www.gotomeeting.com you can set up virtual meetings with slides and video. Skype now allows you to present a video from your computer and get it projected into meeting rooms across the country. The leadership challenge for the generations in remote offices is to keep employees engaged and connected. Here are a few must-haves:

Travel budget: Plan to see employees at least a few times a year.

Technology budget: Don't fall for every fad, but plan to add new tools as they gain traction. Research the technologies that best connect people for the types of work they do.

Routine: Consistency in your work process—quarterly gatherings, weekly phone meetings—provides structure and prevents gaps in communication. Set aside time for regular travel and update calls and be available for people in different time zones.

Drive: Members of dispersed teams need to work well on their own. Their managers need to sustain the group's energy, be available at odd hours, travel a lot and initiate communication.

Chatter: It gets a bad rap, but chit-chat builds a team. Let remote employees in on tidbits like promotions, births and weddings and inside jokes from other offices.

The principles of managing a remote team are similar to good leadership in general; however, it requires more diligence. Here are some steps to take to ensure all of the generations remain connected to the business:

- ✓ A strong team starts with you. You need to show commitment to the remote situation and be committed to be available to the remote team.
- ✓ Choose the right people to work remotely: self starters, results-oriented, almost entrepreneurial in their outlook.
- ✓ Get creative with your existing technology. For example, Louisville, KY-based public relations firm Corecubed records conference call brainstorming sessions so that participants can truly free-flow their thoughts. "No one's taking notes, everyone's being creative, so it's great to have that follow-up," says Corecubed managing director Merrily Orsini. She paid $150 at Radio Shack for a digital voice recorder that connects to her telephone handset. Her administrative assistant downloads the recordings to Corecubed's intranet site, then transcribes them. Employees refer back to the sessions to refresh their memories on a topic or check who's responsible for which tasks.
- ✓ Set up support systems. Know who will take responsibility for technical problems on the remote end. This applies particularly to home-based employees and contractors. At Alpine Access, a Denver-based virtual call center, technical help has been streamlined for its home-based agents. "We have a technical support desk that's able to fix 90 to 95 percent of computer problems over the Internet," says CEO Chris Carrington. For problems that can't be fixed virtually, Alpine will FedEx a new thin-client computer to the agent's home. Carrington says he'd rather retain the best workers than require, as some companies do, that their remote workers live within a short drive of company headquarters.

80: Work Volume

One of the questions I often get from a Zoomer is, "Who is going to do all the work if Gen Y doesn't want to work as hard as we did or do?"

This is a huge concern for the Zoomers, who are looking ahead to post-recession times. If recent data is accurate there is a claim that Gen X will be making a mass exodus from unfulfilling jobs and unhappy workplaces as soon as the economy turns. Just today I spoke to a group of HR leaders in education. The education industry, along with the health industry, is going to experience some of the biggest challenges with a Gen X exodus because of substantive changes within these industries and little innovation (at least at the speed that Gen X would like to see). So an interesting dynamic has been created in the current recession. We all thought that Zoomers would be retiring *en masse* when in fact the Zoomers are going to stick around longer than expected. However, unsatisfied Gen Xs are going to pursue work they love.

Companies can expect greater pain when the economy does revive itself because every generation will be looking at whether they are happy at work and this alone will determine whether they stay or go.

This requires a major transformation in how work volumes are managed. Technology can be creatively used to reduce work volumes but we also need to be willing to look at how things have been done and what we can do to shift efficiencies to reduce work volumes.

Let's look at the generational mindsets around work volume to see where beliefs can prevent us from addressing the bigger picture of how we adjust work to keep everyone as happy as we can.

Zoomers are workhorses and proud of it! You will often hear war stories of how hard they had to work to get where they are or how success only happens when you work hard. Up until now Zoomers have willingly accepted increased work volumes without pushing back because they are hardwired to accept hard work as something they cannot change.

Gen X has had to work as hard as the Zoomers but secretly resent the way they are told to work. I am thinking of a Gen X team member with my company who got phenomenal results in her own way but when she was asked to work a little differently by her Zoomer boss she eventually left the company. Gen Xs believe in the power of planning, strategy and technology to streamline project completion. They do not believe that work volume equates to heroism; in fact, they think it's a sacrifice that Zoomers make to the detriment of their families.

Gen Ys generally do not do well with big piles of work. They get frustrated, depressed and apathetic. Gen Ys prefer to be given work in segments or project pieces so they can feel a sense of accomplishment. They do not see hard work as smart—they see it as stupid. They are so technologically adept that they see technology as a solution to reduce work volumes and get work done efficiently.

So to answer the question, "Who will get the volume of work done?" I say the work will get done but in new efficient ways—with technology, collaboration and creativity.

81: GOALS

Ask any Zoomer how to set goals and they will likely say you must be *smart* when setting goals:

Specific
Measurable
Action oriented
Results oriented
Timely.

Ask Gen X and they will say you set big and lofty goals and write a plan with project pieces and check off the success markers.

Ask a Gen Y and they will say you just decide you want something and everyone around you will help to bring it to fruition.

If you have a Gen Y child you know exactly what I am saying. Zoomers have done the MBAs and the PhDs and they believe you have to have a formula and a method to achieve what you want. Gen Y has had most things done for them so of course their belief system is that things come easily and just as they need them.

Let me give you a personal example. My husband Reg and I decided to move out—I mentioned this earlier. We felt so guilty moving we helped Courtney find an apartment, secure it, set up her electricity, set up her cable, get her insurance, move in—well, you get the picture. We did everything for her! When I moved out my dad said, "See you, and don't come back."

I see goal setting of the future to be purely technical and collaborative. You can use goal-setting software to plunk in your personal goals and it will calculate what your actions, timeline, etc. need to be to get what you want. If any of you have tried to lose weight the technology to support your efforts is already out there. Go to www.weightwatchers. com and you can plunk in your existing weight, your goal weight and bingo! Everything you need to do is provided to you.

Imagine being a Gen Y who downloads an app to save, say, $10,000.00. Every thirty days the app tells them how much money needs to go in the bank account and what timeframe it will take them to reach their goal.

We will also see visual team goal planning software, where everyone keys in their team's contribution to the goal and the computer spits out action lists for the team, points out the hiccups or faults in the project and acts as a virtual goal project manager. Best Buy already has something called Tag Trade, where project managers from different departments input all of the details of various projects they are working on and other leaders get to rate the likelihood of success for the project. Then they compare their predictions with the computer's calculations.

This isn't your parents' goal setting. This is 2020 goal setting using technology to its fullest ability.

82: GLOBALIZATION

Globalization is a relatively new concept for businesses. It emerged late in the 20th century, perhaps when humans first saw images of the Earth from space—a small blue-green planet devoid of boundaries and arbitrary political divisions. Regardless of their novelty, global issues are so important that they may literally determine the future of the human species. Global issues have an impact on virtually all social, environmental, economic, health and security concerns. And those concerns are in themselves global issues. Perhaps one of the most important roles that businesses have today is understanding global issues and the importance to all of the generations of seeing the global connections in how we do business.

Gen Y has an innate sense of global impact because the educational system supported global awareness in the school curriculum. Add to that instant media access, which is how today's Gen Ys were exposed to Columbine, 9/11 and other global events. They have a deep empathetic connection to what is going on in the world and they want the companies they work for to make a global difference.

Media has also opened the eyes of all of the generations—we can see the inequities of pay and labor in other parts of the world. I predict an equalization of income for the poorest countries that currently provide goods and services for the rest of the world. Consumer awareness has increased to the point that a friend of mine, Stephen Hammond, the author of *Human Rights at Work*, refuses to buy anything made in China. Companies are listening to their consumers more and more and therefore employees of those companies want to do what's right for the globe, not just for the profits of their organizations.

From an employee's perspective here is how each of the generations looks at global companies:

Zoomers look at increased market share, increased opportunities to diversify and increased ability to leverage changing economic conditions across the globe. On a personal level they find global organizations appealing because they see future prospects for contract work upon retirement or for moving their families to another country for the experience.

Gen X sees increased competitive advantage, increased upward mobility and promotion opportunities. Gen X is more than willing to move to another country for work, and sees globalization in the context of increased ability to gain education and invaluable experience in another country.

Globalization holds a huge attraction for Gen Y in regards to choosing to work for a company. They are globetrotters and globally interested. They want to work for companies who are doing global good so companies that are doing projects in Haiti or building homes with Habitat for Humanity hold great appeal for Gen Y.

83: Teamwork

I have tried to ensure that I cover most of the areas of work that are affected by the dynamics of multiple generations in the workplace. One of the biggest opportunities for business owners and leaders is to put continued focus and efforts in helping multigenerational teams understand each other and then take informed action to create better overall results. We can take fundamental actions to increase the desire of each generation to work better as a team.

Here's a look at what will assist us in providing incentives for each of the generations to be a team player. Let's start with Gen Y:

- ✓ Trust Gen Ys with challenge and responsibility, including special assignments.
- ✓ Create an internship program that focuses on giving them meaningful work.
- ✓ Let interns come up with their own training topics and invite senior staff to attend and take part in discussions.
- ✓ Involve them as the technical experts for the team and rely on this strength.
- ✓ Appoint on-boarding or orientation sponsors to make contact with new hires prior to their first day on the job.
- ✓ Require younger staff to give frequent presentations to the team.
- ✓ Encourage senior staff to initiate more face-to-face communication with them.
- ✓ Use strength and personality assessment instruments to increase self-awareness.

- ✓ Provide ample opportunities for learning in a variety of media—online, via podcasts or files on thumb drives, over lunch-and-learns, in classes and from varied work experiences.
- ✓ Involve them in more direct contact with internal and external customers so they better understand why their jobs are important.
- ✓ Set up office spaces to facilitate social interaction and exchange of ideas.
- ✓ Consider assigning workstations in closer proximity to more senior employees.

For Gen X:

- ✓ Create opportunities to move cross-functionally and provide rotational and other special assignments, especially when the path to promotion is blocked.
- ✓ Assign them team tasks that give them company profile and senior management recognition.
- ✓ Put them in charge or as a mentor of Gen Ys and let them do it their own way.
- ✓ Conduct assessment and training seminars for the emerging leaders among them.
- ✓ Involve them in succession management discussions.
- ✓ Allow flexible hours whenever possible as long as the work gets done.
- ✓ Reward those who make personal and family sacrifices to achieve team goals.
- ✓ Challenge them to create a new job for themselves by identifying unmet needs or problems that their skills and strengths can help solve.

And for Zoomers:

- ✓ Train them in more a "hands-on" coaching style of management, including a focus on setting shorter-term goals for younger staff and rewarding small successes along the way to sustain their interest and engagement.
- ✓ Have them mentor technically competent Gen Xers who need to develop better interpersonal skills and political subtleties.

- ✓ Assign every Zoomer manager to a Gen Xer or Millennial to mentor and help him or her develop a career plan.
- ✓ Identify Zoomer "early adopters" of newer technologies (who can usually relate better to their peers) and let them teach their colleagues. They may be able to do this more effectively than younger staff.
- ✓ Re-energize them by challenging them to learn new subjects or take on new projects that tap hidden strengths they have not previously used.
- ✓ Re-engage Zoomers on the cusp of retirement by challenging them to pass on their knowledge and leave a legacy through mentorship.

84: ACCOUNTABILITY

At this point in the book you may be feeling as though there is no accountability for the Gen X or Gen Y generations. You may be a Zoomer who feels that you will continue to have to work hard and be in charge while the other generations slack off and get to have a life. Not so!

We can instill personal accountability in each of the generations. We just need to understand their thinking and adapt our communication to motivate them to want to take personal accountability. By the way, accountability is not limited to specific generations, nor are many of the items in this book. We are simply looking at it from the generational viewpoint so that we can take that into consideration when approaching our team members.

Gen Y is far more comfortable being part of a team and being made accountable to a team. If they feel they are part of something larger than themselves, that they must have a commitment to the team and its results, you will find Gen Ys will generally step up and be accountable. They are less likely to want to be solely responsible for the success of a project—they would much rather share the accolades with the team than be singled out. With a Gen Y who does not want to be accountable you need to communicate the merits and the consequences of their actions. In my experience Gen Y wants to make their bosses happy; they just need a little handholding to give you what you are looking for.

Gen X are used to being held accountable but you have to talk to a Gen X in very direct terms and let them know the consequences of not doing it the way it has been set up. You have to be careful, though, because if you are too aggressive and don't show them respect or appreciation they will jump ship as soon as they have the chance. It's almost a passive-aggressive response, where the psychological response is, "I won't get mad now, I will get even later." We want to avoid pushing Gen X to respond in subconsciously passive-aggressive ways. I said earlier that you have to be direct with Gen X but if you use the "my way or the highway" approach with them they will do it your way while plotting their eventual escape.

I mentioned in another chapter the story about the Gen X who worked in a remote office for a sales company. She was very good at her job but didn't want to have to increase her cold calls. When her Zoomer boss asked her to add a weekly report showing her cold call activity she balked. She didn't feel she should have to prove her work. In reality the Zoomer was asking for performance tracking and when she pushed the request with the Gen X it became an issue. Eventually the Gen X quit the job because she felt that she was being micro-managed. The truth is the Gen X did not want to have to change how she was doing her job and the Zoomer felt she had to show performance results for the company. The Gen X was not willing to be held accountable.

Zoomers need to share their personal responsibility. I believe Zoomers have established a pattern of doing so much on their own, taking on more projects and having the attitude of "if I don't do it, who will?" If you have set the pattern of always being the one to do it, then guess what? Everyone else says to himself or herself, "Okay, fly at it!" Then the Zoomer gets bitter and angry at having to work so hard. Zoomers need to share what they know, share the responsibilities, learn how to manage others to perform a task or job and hold their employees accountable for their performance once they've been taught.

Accountability is a two-way street. We need to be personally accountable and we have to be willing and able to hold others accountable as well.

85: Multiple Languages

As the economy recovers we can expect to see more companies attracting multilingual employees. Where English was once the dominant language in the workplace many companies in California now have Spanish-speaking employees as the majority.

Many Gen X and Gen Y are proficient at more than one language—their Zoomer parents wanted to ensure they would have a competitive advantage when they entered the workforce. Many Zoomers are learning a second language to increase their abilities and in response to the multilingual Gen X and Gen Ys.

If language is a barrier or a challenge for you and your company it seems technology is going to assist us once again. PDA and iPhone apps now make it possible to have instant translation, which speeds up communication and helps bridge language gaps.

I predict in the next five to ten years we will completely erode the language barrier as technology increases the ability for instant translation through Bluetooth-like devices or even an around the neck voice translator. Think of the implications for the workplace if you are a leader and you could instantly understand your Spanish-speaking employees.

Whether it's *parlez-vous français*, *habla español* or *você fala português*, more American companies are looking to recruit and hire bilingual or multilingual employees. Several factors contribute to this trend, but there are two primary reasons for the increased need to recruit multilingual employees. They are:

1. A growing immigrant population in the US that is not fluent in English

2. American companies becoming more global—expanding their operations oversees, which requires employees to speak another language.

"Over the past two to three years, we have seen an increase in companies asking us for employees that have a language besides English," says Teresa Setting, vice president of recruiting and retention at Troy, MI-based Kelly Services, a temporary employment and staffing firm. "We're finding that more companies are becoming global, and, as the US population diversifies, companies want to market to these ethnic groups."

Demand is primarily increasing within the pharmaceutical, life sciences, technology and financial services sectors for managerial candidates with bilingual skills, according to Chris van Someren, president of global markets at Los Angeles-based Korn/Ferry International, which specializes in executive recruitment. This need can be attributed to the increasing global presence of US companies. More American firms have divisions or manufacturing facilities overseas.

In the United States, the greatest need for bilingual employees is in the consumer services sector, in such areas as banking, retailing and telecommunications. Within these industries, bilingual employees are needed to fill positions such as call or customer service center personnel, receptionists and secretaries and medical and legal administrative staff.

86: Work From Home

I have talked throughout this book about Gen X's great desire for work flexibility around their families and Gen Y's keen desire to have flexibility for play time. Well, Zoomers are now on the bandwagon—they want to be able to have the flexibility to work from home too.

For decades in North American households the most dreaded morning sound has been that of an alarm clock. Sometime between six and seven AM a beep or radio music signaled that it was time to get up and head to work. But in the early 21st century two things have begun to change. First, the alarm clock is going off a little bit later. And second, instead of putting on suits and driving to work, people are heading to the basement or den in their pajamas and turning on their personal computers. These are the early days of the new Work From Home generation.

With the invention of modern laptops, broadband Internet access and advances in communication software, there is no longer a need to be in the office. At least not every day. Thousands of companies are rolling out work from home policies and hundreds of thousands of people are starting to take advantage of them. What are the pros and cons of working from home?

If you live in the suburbs and work in the city, it likely takes you thirty minutes or more each day to get to and from work. In particularly busy metropolitan areas like New York, Washington, DC or Atlanta you are lucky if your commute is under an hour each way. Commuting takes time and energy (spending time in traffic is particularly draining). It is routine and boring and rarely productive or relaxing. Not commuting simply means more time to do things that you could not do otherwise.

In addition to being able to spend more time with the family, having no commute has another big benefit—financial savings. With the cost of gasoline going through the roof, not having to drive is important for everyone. And we are talking big savings. If a tank of gas costs you $50 and lasts a week, cutting that in half gets you a cool $100 a month. The work-from-home folks also save money on food. Even in the cheapest corporate cafeterias lunch is generally going to cost around $7. At home, if you are stingy, you can spend $2 on a tasty lunch. This is easily another $100 per month in savings.

Working from home also has a global environmental benefit. By commuting less we save energy and reduce pollution. This is one of those rare moments when humans are in harmony with the planet— what is good for us is good for the environment as well.

Perhaps one of the most surprising benefits of working from home is that it can actually increase productivity. Assuming that your home office environment is conducive to work and you are able to focus, more work is going to get done. If you can't focus on work with home distractions (kids, the lure of daytime TV, etc.) you may want to rethink working at home in the first place.

A typical office environment is noisy: people are talking, phones are ringing, co-workers are coming by to chat and there are always crowds near the coffee and soda machines. At home these distractions are not going to be present. In addition, when working from home you will be focused more on your work instead of office politics. Playing politics and kissing up to the boss is not easily done over the phone, so people will get more work done instead.

87: Time Management

It seems fitting that the preceding chapter is about working from home because those who do so successfully have mastered the art of time management.

Studies show that people who work from home are more productive because they tend to work longer than they would at the office. It's called "not-being-in-the-office guilt." The generations hold wildly different viewpoints on how one should manage time. The bottom line is to ask, "Is the project or assignment getting done in the timeframe allotted?" If it is, then it really doesn't matter how it got done or how the person managed their time. Instead of looking at time management from solely a generational viewpoint let's look at time management "personalities."

1. Use notes and checklists that act as reminders.

People who favor this approach believe in managing their time by writing notes and creating checklists of things to be done. This method of time management is favored by Zoomers because they were educated in time management using the datebook method created by Stephen Covey in the early '80s. The items on the list are not arranged by priority—the note simply acts as a reminder of all the tasks that must be completed during the day. By following the checklist and marking off tasks as they are accomplished, such people are able to keep track of everything that needs to be completed. Tasks not completed within the stipulated time are put on the next day's list.

2. Prepare and plan using calendars and PDAs.

Time managers of the Gen X generation typically favor constructive planning and like to be prepared well in advance by scheduling their tasks. Such people use scheduling materials such as calendars and the computer to write down the times and venues of meetings and important events, etc. They use Outlook, ICalendar or Google Calendar along with BlackBerrys and other PDAs.

3. Project approach.

Zoomers and Gen X can take the entire time management activity to the next level by identifying those tasks that must be completed first. Arranging activities of the day on a priority basis helps them to set different time goals. Such people may maintain their task list on the computer or in hard copy (organizer or appointment book). They may use technology to remind them with pre-set alarms in their calendars to remind them of appointments or tasks. They use the voice recorder option on their PDAs to save time when planning a follow-up task.

4. Efficient and proactive.

Those who use this type of time management understand and appreciate the difference between urgent and important tasks. In our attempt to accomplish urgent tasks we often ignore those activities that are of utmost importance. Such an approach can prove to be very costly in the long run as it makes us forget about things that are important in our lives and need our time, simply because they are not urgent! This is where a Zoomer can get into conflict with a Gen Y because a Gen Y may not know all of the history of a project or task. Therefore they do not have the advantage of being able to be proactive.

5. Technical time management geeks.

This group of people uses technology to the highest level to help them manage their time and projects. Often Gen Ys are excellent at time management because they use their technology to its fullest abilities. They take their laptops with them to write reports or documents while at the coffee shop. They use their PDA to call, e-mail, text or IM someone who needs an immediate answer. They use the GPS on their PDAs to give them walking or driving instructions. They look in advance at how much travel time they can expect. They use shared calendars so that teams know where they are and others can put schedule items into their calendars. They set up auto-responses on their e-mail to direct people to other options. They use Skype to talk to their global partners and online meeting tools to obtain group consensus quickly.

They easily jump from task to task and, although it may seem like they are not managing their time well, they end up meeting the deadline.

88: PRIORITIES

Ask Zoomers about prioritization in the workplace and they will express frustration that their employees or team members don't seem to have the same priorities as they do. Or they feel that others don't know how to set priorities that are in line with the team's goals. Quite simply, setting priorities is all about communication. If we are not continually communicating the company's vision, mission and goals, and coaching our teams to think of these things when setting their priorities then we are setting ourselves up for disappointment.

In my consulting experience, what one person sees as a priority is not how another person may see it. Zoomer leaders need to invest time in handholding and guiding their Gen X and Gen Y employees to set priorities based on what they deem high priority. By the same token I encourage Gen X and Gen Y to openly communicate what they have on their plates to their Zoomer bosses so that any barriers to completing their top priority tasks can be addressed and possibly removed.

A great example of communicating priorities is a consulting client of mine where the VP of operations and the general manager were having conflict over what each of them deemed to be most important. The VP of operations (a Gen X) often presented proposals to government groups aimed at getting their company included on the government's preferred vendor list. The VP of operations would delegate the preparation of the proposal to the general manager (a Gen Y).

On one follow up consulting visit I was talking with the general manager and she complained that the VP of operations' priorities were not hers. When I asked investigative questions it turned out that the VP had never communicated what priority the proposals had in relation to the other projects the general manager had on her plate. He would give her arbitrary urgent deadlines without explaining or asking how this would fit in to the GM's schedule.

I did point out to the GM that it was her responsibility to communicate to her VP what other projects she had and their order of priority. It is important to know that setting priorities does not rest solely with the delegator in this scenario. Both parties need to negotiate timelines and clearly communicate expectations so that there is clear agreement on the priorities.

When setting our own priorities we need to ask ourselves the following questions:

- ✓ What do I have to accomplish this month, week or day?
- ✓ What is the most urgent item that is most crucial to overall company benefit?
- ✓ What do I have to have done by the end of the day, knowing I will have multiple interruptions?
- ✓ What would make the most impact for my boss and his or her objectives?

When delegating priorities we need to ask the following questions to the person we asking to do the task:

- ✓ What do you have going on this month, week or day?
- ✓ Can you please make this request your top priority for today?
- ✓ Who can help you with this?
- ✓ If you can't get this to me today can you get it to me by end of day tomorrow?

Again, it is about communicating expectations. If you find yourself frustrated with someone else not understanding priorities then it is your responsibility to take the time to help them understand.

89: HEALTH BENEFITS

Aside from their approaches to technology, some of the greatest differences between Gen X, Gen Y and the Zoomers can be seen in the benefits they seek. Employees from the Zoomer generation typically have been in the workforce longer, know exactly what they want when it comes to health coverage and may make employment decisions based on that information. Younger generations may be less likely to have pre-existing medical conditions, may not see the need for specialized care, may be on their parents' plan or have gotten by with minimal or no coverage in college. They may be less familiar with the cost of health care and individual services through lack of necessity.

Those from Generation Y may be more concerned with gaining experience and getting their feet wet. They may prefer higher salaries over benefits, since many are just starting out, paying back college tuition, and often living paycheck to paycheck between car loans and first apartment rent.

A lot of Gen Ys want to get into the reality TV industry. A large production company in the reality TV industry has offered subsidized health insurance to all of its production employees, when many in the reality industry do not.

Unlike their Zoomer counterparts, who are more likely to embrace traditional or defined plans, Gen Y employees may be more willing to consider Health Savings Accounts (HSAs) that combine high-deductible health insurance with a tax-free savings account. They may also consider other plans to make basic coverage more attainable.

Two and a half years ago, Pie Town Productions, a TV production company with offices in LA and Chicago, decided to also offer employees a Health Maintenance Organization (HMO)-based plan. "It was 50–50 then," their HR director said. "Now, it's 30–70 in favor of HMO, regardless of generation, because those with families can get the HMO for their family for the cost of a Preferred Provider Organization (PPO) covering just a couple. The HMO for a single individual is 30 percent of the cost of the PPO, the main benefits to the PPO being greater access and no referral required."

In regards to dental it is likely that a Gen Y would most likely stick to a less expensive plan. They might still have a plan through their parents or are just using dental once a year for cleaning.

More employees in general seem to be looking to go to the PPO, since stand-alone medical and dental are not linked. Often PPOs can be three times the cost of HMOs but they give the company and the employees more provider options.

Zoomers and Gen X with children are looking for quality in medical benefits plans, because they need regular appointments, medication coverage and greater peace of mind. Most employers are happy to comply with their employees' desires for increased coverage.

Gen X and Y are also looking at alternative health care as being part of their medical coverage. In Canada many companies are offering reimbursement for acupuncture, massage and other complementary health options.

Providing the most flexible options in regards to health benefits will prove to be a competitive advantage for employers. Each of the generations has unique medical and dental requirements and they want plans and options that suit their stage of life.

90: PERKS

I mentioned earlier in the compensation and recognition sections of the book that there are certain perks that appeal specifically to Gen Y.

Fortune magazine recently named Google the number-one company to work for, a ranking based largely on Google's well-publicized employee perks: free meals in its gourmet cafeteria; on-site doctors, dry cleaners and gym facilities; and even a policy that allows employees to bring their pets to work. Here are some more perks offered by Google—perhaps your company will not go to this extent but it gives you a sense of what kind of workplace would offer these perks:

1. Google provides free custom detailing on all employee-owned Segways, motorized scooters, recumbent bicycles and other green modes of transportation.

2. For recent computer science grads accepting an engineering position with Google, a popular social event is "New Employee Orientation." It is a social event, not a formal employee orientation!

3. Google employees who are about to become mothers receive twelve weeks of maternity leave.

4. Googlers enjoy an Employee Referral Program, meaning they receive a cash bonus if they refer management to any employee even thinking about leaving Google. This is a great retention strategy.

7. Google employees can commute to work via free company shuttle.

8. To encourage collaboration, the hallways at Google are lined with whiteboards where employees can jot down ideas.

9. Google engineers make use of free on-site hair salons.
10. Google has a beach volleyball site.
11. Following its acquisition of YouTube, Google began arranging employee tours of YouTube headquarters.
12. Google has on-site baristas to make lattés and other specialty drinks.
13. Google engineers are given "20 percent time" in which they are free to pursue their own personal projects 20 percent of the time. This incentive has produced such efforts as Gmail and Google News.
14. Google provides free financial planning classes to all its employees.

91: Financial Planning

When I was in banking the common advice of the time (the mid '80s to the early '90s) was to get a good job, stay there, shore up your pension and then one day you could retire. For me, born on the Gen X–Zoomer cusp, this notion never quite sat well because while I had been at the bank we had gone through three or four restructures. When I left the bank in the early '90s my boss asked me why I would give up my pension. I was twenty-eight years old and I just didn't see the sense in hanging around for something that might or might not provide for me in my retirement years. I was wired to create wealth through self-employment and shrewd investments with a few risks mixed in. Little did I know that I was ahead of my time in regards to financial planning.

Many Zoomers today are faced with having to start over with their finances due to many factors: divorce, job loss and investment failure, to name a few. The recent economic meltdown has forced many Zoomers to remain in the workforce longer than they planned. Another factor is that Gen Ys are staying home longer so the Zoomers are supporting them into their early thirties. Financially Zoomers have to continue working to maintain the lifestyle they have achieved for themselves and their families.

So let's look at how each of the generations looks at finances presently and into the future.

I am quite surprised by the financial maturity of many Gen Ys that I have worked with, including my own daughter Courtney. Gen Ys are actually quite pragmatic with their money. They do like nice things and tend to want the designer goods that they see in the media and on reality TV. The luxury goods industry has recognized that Gen Y is their future market so they have made their products far more accessible than was ever possible for Gen X or Zoomers. In fact, if a Gen Y can't afford to buy the latest designer handbag they can rent it from one of many online sites for a special occasion. Remember, Gen Y has always banked online.

From an employer's standpoint Gen Y is looking for good pay with flexibility and they also want to enjoy the benefits of travel and perks, as I mentioned earlier. They are less likely to put their money into an RRSP but more likely to want to buy a first home at a young age. Their parents are in most cases helping them go to school so the money they earn is for their own use or for their future.

Many Gen Xs lost investment money in the stock market fallout and they too are regrouping. Money they thought they had in stocks or investments is no longer there. They are looking at planning for their children's education and purchasing a home. They are less likely to put a lot of their money into RRSPs and more likely to use it for investments in revenue property or savings. Credit card use is high with this demographic but they are also likely to pay off their monthly balances. Employers that offer dollar-for-dollar profit sharing options, pension matching or free financial planners are highly attractive to Gen X.

As Zoomers work to recover the losses they incurred in the recent economic turmoil they are looking to invest in more solid ventures. Many Zoomers are purchasing vacation properties or are looking at revenue properties for their retirement income. Companies that recognize Zoomers are looking for contract work or outsourced project work that lets them semi-retire will be very attractive to the Zoomer. The Zoomer is also looking at alternative retirement options, such as working part time until they are in their mid-seventies. Many Zoomers are also looking at investing in businesses rather than stocks.

Suggestions for companies for all of the generations:
- ✓ Offer financial planning as part of your benefits or perks
- ✓ If you have profit sharing, ensure all employees take advantage of it and know it is available
- ✓ When working on incentives for your employees recognize the unique financial stages each of the generations is in
- ✓ Zoomers especially are willing to exchange time for money. Come up with unique ways to provide time in lieu of money.
- ✓ Provide confidential credit counselling to employees as a benefit or perk.

92: STRATEGIC PLANNING

Recently I facilitated a one-day strategic planning session with Gen X and Gen Y leaders. When I was asked by the CEO to facilitate this session he sheepishly admitted that in the past he and his partner did all of the strategic planning and then force-fed it to his leaders, hoping that they would embrace it and run with it. What he realized was that to go from $3 million a year to $10 million he needed to empower and include his department leaders.

That's where I came in. It was evident to me on the day everyone arrived for the strategic planning session that they were nervous and dubious about being included. They thought it was a trap!

I structured the format to have the two owners talk about where the company has been, where it is now and where they want it to go. This alone was eye-opening for the leaders around the table so when we got into asking for their input to achieve the vision they were still a little shy and reluctant to contribute.

I facilitated an exercise where the owners confessed their fears about not achieving the vision and what they promise to do and be as the company moves forward. This opened the door for trust in the process and by the end of the day we had a compelling strategic vision and plan that each and every Gen X and Gen Y was eager to be a part of.

The road to 2020 requires greater collaboration, and must include an invitation to all of the stakeholders in the planning process. Gone are the days where the leaders can arbitrarily say what the future is going to be and then expect their leadership team to implement it without any buy-in.

Here's how to include the generations in your next strategic planning process:

- ✓ Prepare a pre-planning survey to gather insights, moods and ideas prior to the actual planned strategic planning session (I use the online tool SurveyMonkey, which is very easy to use and good for gathering data).
- ✓ Leave the ego outside. In an effective strategic planning session the majority stakeholders such as the owners or the department heads need to park their egos at the door and be fully present, listen carefully and be open to ideas presented.
- ✓ Encourage everyone to present ideas and to voice concerns without repercussions.
- ✓ Reward collaboration and ideas. When I facilitate strategic planning retreats I always insist the retreat be offsite, away from the office, with perks such as Starbucks lattés, a nice lunch—and in a two or three-day retreat a fun group activity such as mini-golf or ziplining.
- ✓ Invest time prior to the strategic planning retreat to talk to everyone face to face before attending the session. By taking the time to encourage participation and ask for ideas you are showing respect for their input, which will increase their participation.
- ✓ Ensure that the strategic plan is captured immediately. Put it in a PDF document and send it to the participants as soon as possible. I recommend you do this in the first few days after the retreat; otherwise you risk losing the energy and ideas from the planning session.
- ✓ Hire a professional (outside) facilitator. Research shows that outsourcing facilitation allows all stakeholders to participate at the same level. If senior management or executives facilitate the event you will not get the same level of openness or contribution.

93: PROFIT SHARING

Profit sharing refers to monetary benefits offered to employees by the employer apart from salary and bonuses. It is a form of incentive given to employees either directly or indirectly, depending upon the pre-tax profits made by the company. The profit can be shared with eligible employees in the form of bonds, stocks or cash, which can be disbursed at the time of retirement or immediately. The company takes the base salary of each employee into consideration, and those employees with higher base salaries will get a larger share of the available profit.

Profit sharing is a gesture extended by a company to make employees feel that they are part of the company's success. Any employee who is well taken care of will perform better. His or her motivation to work will be higher.

Advantages of profit sharing:
- ✓ Brings employees together to work toward a common goal.
- ✓ Motivation levels will be high.
- ✓ Employees' focus is on profitability.
- ✓ Increases employees' commitment to the organization.
- ✓ Employees can identify with the company. They feel part of its success.
- ✓ Bridges the gap between the employee and employer.
- ✓ Promotes the wellbeing of the employee.
- ✓ Additional income allows the employee to lead a comfortable life.

Disadvantages of profit sharing:
- ✓ Salaries of individual employees go up equally, not on the basis of merit or promotion.

✓ In the case of smaller companies drastic fluctuations in the earnings of the company may affect the personal earnings of the employees. For example, you could have a remarkable year where profits are way up and everyone gets a huge payout and then follow that with a bad year in which everyone does not get a bonus or payout.

✓ The focus of the employee may be on profit instead of on quality.

Employees like to have shares in the profits of the company. It is some kind of reward for their hard work and efforts. They are motivated to put in their best efforts.

According to the responses of some 700 companies that have implemented profit-sharing schemes, financial participation in particular serves as an incentive device for workers. A large majority (almost 85 percent) of companies aims to raise effort, productivity and/or creativity levels of their employees (see table below). Moreover, profit sharing is used as a tool to increase the willingness of workers to adapt to change.

Reasons for profit sharing	% of companies
Incentive device	84.7
Recruitment and retaining (specific) employees	25.2
Wage fairness considerations	19.5
Improving workplace atmosphere	16.9
Management by objectives	11.5
Safeguarding jobs	8.8

Note: Multiple responses given; 704 companies responded to the survey item on reason for introducing profit sharing. Source: IW Köln Economic Research Institute, 2007

Overall, over a quarter of the companies surveyed use profit sharing as a device to recruit or to retain employees. Not surprisingly, this applies particularly to companies with schemes exclusively provided for selected individuals, such as managers. One out of five respondents aims to institute a fair wage structure as well as a reasonable distribution of revenues between owners and employees. Interestingly, the motive of "safeguarding jobs" is of minor significance. This implies that companies are not primarily interested in transferring risks that arise from a volatile environment to their employees.

94: Restructures & Acquisitions

Zoomers and Gen X may well remember the economy in the early '80s. Interest rates were as high as 22 percent and people were losing their homes in one of the nation's ugliest recessions. Zoomers and Gen X have also been through high levels of instability in their work as companies have experienced massive change, restructures and acquisitions. If the current economy is any indicator we are going to see even more major restructuring and amalgamations of organizations.

Gen Ys are having their first experience with a recession but it is affecting them differently than their parents or their Gen X counterparts. I know that after I left the bank to work for a private insurance company in the early '90s they went through a major downsize: they laid off 50 percent of their employees across the country. I was asked to stay and help manage the downsizing and that experience is what led me to self-employment. I realized that I didn't want my job security to be at the whim of an organization. My father had been an entrepreneur, so for me the restructuring was a gift. It caused me to set out on my own about a year after it happened.

Having managed a few restructurings in my finance career and also as a consultant for my corporate and small business clients, I have found a successful restructuring really comes down to adaptability to change. The more set we are in our ways or the longer we have been entrenched in a situation the more difficult it is to accept change.

A few days ago I was keynoting at a HR conference for CUPA (College and Universities Professional Association) and my keynote was called "Take Positive Control of the Future." In the keynote I said that the main demographic holding innovation back is the Zoomers. Yes, I am saying that restructuring and acquisitions do lead to innovation—change is forced and it causes everyone to have to find new ways to adapt, get the work done and use technology more effectively. Many Zoomers resist this process.

Of course this ticked off a few Zoomers but when I pointed out the gains that Gen X and Gen Y are trying to make and the resistance they get from the Zoomers I got nods of agreement. After the keynote I had a Gen Y approach me in tears. She was tasked with a major technology project and she said that every day was a battle to get the Zoomers on side.

Here are my do's and don'ts for successful restructuring and acquisitions (at least the people part).

Do's	Don'ts
Train all staff in change management	Expect everyone to get it
Get senior management to endorse Gen Y tech projects	Be negative about the change
Have a company-wide meeting on details	Keep information quiet
Keep the stakeholders informed	Withhold key details
Outline who is acquiring who and what it means	Pretend it's all okay
Introduce departments to their new counterparts in the other company	Keep companies separate
Keep everyone in the loop with weekly updates	Communicate once
Engage the generations in dialogue and ideas	Ignore ideas and suggestions
Be honest about job losses and changes	Sugar-coat the facts
Help people find new positions	Let them find their own way
Hire a consultant to provide an objective perspective on the change	Use clichés or pat answers

95: Definition of Busy

I get quite passionate when I talk about this subject. In today's society it is almost a badge of honor to brag about how busy we are. You hear people say, "I am so busy," as if this makes them important and somewhat superior to people who aren't busy. When I hear the phrase "I am so busy" from my clients I always ask, "Doing what?" Then I get them to list all of the things they have going on. By the time we write it all down it turns out that many activities overlap so, in reality, they have not set up their day or their tasks to meet their deadlines. Instead they procrastinate or delegate without follow-up, which causes them undue stress. Let's look at some generational definitions of "busy" and see how we can cut through the BS and create a greater sense of control over time and projects.

Zoomers typically define busy as over-committed and stressed about what they have said "yes" to. Because of the Zoomer work ethic they will take on more than they can reasonably get done and then they feel trapped or resentful because they have little time to relax. But Zoomers can un-learn such behavior. When I was working on this book I had an extremely tight deadline to complete it. A colleague of mine requested that I write some copy for a joint project we were working on and instead of saying yes I said no. She was surprised and a little put out, but I was able to have a very open conversation with her about the fact that I was already under pressure to finish current writing commitments and by saying yes to her I felt that I was over-committing. To her credit, she completely understood and decided to take the first shot at writing up the joint project. She appreciated my honesty. If I had said yes I would have been ticked off at myself for accepting the self-imposed pressure.

I no longer have the need to say how busy I am and I see having more leisure time as a true indicator of my success.

Gen Xs have learned to say no quite well—they aim for quality busy! Gen X doesn't mind taking work home or working from home on the weekend for specific projects because it allows them to fit the work in around their family. Gen Xs use their BlackBerrys and other PDAs like their right hand so they are quite efficient. A Gen X leader of a company I am working with will answer her e-mails late at night because she is a night person and likes getting things like e-mail responses done when she is feeling energized. Compared to a Zoomer who might let their in-box fill up with e-mails, a Gen X handles e-mails in odd moments of the day—while they are in a line-up, while waiting for an appointment or after parking the car. They do not view this as the same kind of intrusion as a Zoomer might. They view it as being efficient with their time.

Gen Y's definition of busy is how much work they can cram into a shorter period of time so that they can have time off. This is why project work is so appealing to Gen Y. They will work hard to get a project completed and then they see no problem in taking a few days off to enjoy some personal time. Where a Zoomer might work hard constantly a Gen Y needs frequent playtime.

So when you hear someone say they are busy, ask them, "Doing what?" You can help them determine where to focus their energy and you can also point out to them that everyone is busy. It's not something that makes them more special than anyone else.

96: CONFIDENCE

In a recent conference keynote I asked the audience about the boundless Gen Y confidence and a bitter Zoomer shouted out, "They think they are all that." Well guess what? Gen Y has innate confidence because we, their parents, have instilled it in them. If we look at how Zoomers were raised compared to the environment of a Gen X or Gen Y you can see where the confidence comes from. For Zoomers the message received during their childhoods was, "Children are to be seen, not heard," and "Don't boast or brag." Many Zoomers learned to hold their tongues and curb their voices. Zoomers were also told to respect their elders and not to speak unless spoken to.

Compare that message with what Gen X or Gen Y heard growing up. In my case my father raised me, which was pretty rare in the mid '60s. He was a strong role model for me in that he always told me I could be and do anything. My father would chastise me if I gave up because of what someone else thought. Because of that I have a fair amount of confidence and even speaking in front of groups, which I have done for more than fifteen years now, was never a big challenge for me. Fast forward to my daughter Courtney, who I mentioned earlier and who is twenty two years old. When she was growing up we told her she was wonderful and smart, she could be and do anything, she should speak up for herself, question authority if she didn't feel comfortable and even negotiate her grades if she wasn't happy with what she got.

Most Gen Ys received that kind of message at home so it's no wonder that they show up at the workplace chock full of confidence. If, as a Zoomer, you resent this you will find it a huge challenge to motivate Gen Xs or Gen Ys with confidence. It is important for Zoomers to celebrate the confidence of Gen X and Y and be thrilled that Gen X and Y have developed such great inner confidence. Instead of shutting it down we need to be secure and well-adapted Zoomers who celebrate their confidence and build on it for increased success.

Great leaders, regardless of their generation, have so much self-confidence that they do not see others with strong confidence as a threat. Rather, they see it as an asset and they coach, build up and guide Gen X and Gen Y to even greater performance and opportunities.

97: Office Romance

A book about the generations and how to understand their different values wouldn't be complete without a look at how each of the generations views office romance.

Here are some interesting statistics from a survey done by Vault. com on office romances:

- ✓ 58 percent of people surveyed have been involved in an office romance.
- ✓ 20 percent surveyed say the shaky economy makes them want to have an office romance.
- ✓ 21 percent of those surveyed have dated their boss or their supervisor.
- ✓ 57 percent surveyed know of a married co-worker who has had an office romance.

Times have indeed changed. Where an office romance was once a scandal it is now almost expected in many workplaces.

Zoomers have been exposed to office romance for a while now and while it always leads to good gossip (unless there is favoritism or unfair practice) most don't care very much. I did have a client whose fiancée was the payroll person, which created discomfort for the rest of the staff. Also, in an attempt to avoid showing favoritism, her boyfriend the boss came down really hard on her and frequently embarrassed her in front of the other staff. My suggestion was that they consider not working together in the company. She found another job and things have calmed down in the office (and, I hope, in the relationship).

It's common for Generation Xs to have met their spouse or partner at work. Let's face it, a lot of us spend the majority of our time there and it seems inevitable that sparks can fly. Gen Y is so exposed to reality TV shows like *Jersey Shore*, where everyone is cheating on everyone else, that they often don't see the problems associated with office romance.

Regardless of generational viewpoints it is important to know the do's and don'ts as a company and as leaders to manage this growing phenomenon.

Do's

- ✓ Make sure you cover office romances in your company handbook and communicate policies to all employees. It can be a distinct policy on its own, or could be included in something like a "Dignity at Work" policy.
- ✓ Ensure that all management staff members are clear on how relationships between employees should be handled.
- ✓ Visibly avoid favouritism. Having a line manager carry out her subordinate partner's pay review isn't likely to be well-received by other team members.
- ✓ Be aware if a relationship breaks down. If one partner is having trouble dealing with the split it could affect productivity, or worse, lead to allegations of harassment.

Don'ts

- ✓ Bury your head in the sand. Workplace romances are becoming more common as people spend more time in the office and company policy must acknowledge that.
- ✓ Take a draconian approach and try to enforce a ban. That risks alienating and demotivating good employees, who may just decide to leave.
- ✓ Allow "pillow talk." Make it clear that any employee in a relationship with a less-senior colleague shouldn't divulge information to which their partner wouldn't otherwise have access.
- ✓ Forget employees are human.

If love is in the air there's very little you can do about it, which is why a sensible policy is the best option.

98: Professionalism

If Gen Ys are asking for a more relaxed and casual work atmosphere where does that leave us in regards to professionalism? What exactly is professionalism and how do we train people in it?

These are the two most common questions I get asked by Zoomer managers and leaders. The Zoomers are looking through their lens of past experience and protocol and they are expecting Gen X and Gen Y to naturally know what it looks like to be professional. Recently I walked into my hair salon and the Gen Y receptionist was having a loud personal conversation on the main phone. It was awkward and unprofessional. Someone needed to have a conversation with her about professional behavior.

What is professional behavior according to Zoomers?

✓ Appropriate dress
✓ Minimal visible piercings and tattoos
✓ No unnecessary skin showing
✓ Focus on the customer. Do not talk to co-workers about negative situations with a customer present.
✓ Don't chew gum loudly.
✓ Polite greetings and responses
✓ No gossip
✓ Do not go over your boss's head
✓ Respect private conversations. Don't repeat sensitive information.
✓ No temper tantrums or displays of disagreement in front of others.
✓ Don't blindside someone before a meeting—have a one-on-one if the information is going to be related to that individual.

✓ Don't badmouth the company, the employees or their policies to the customer

It is necessary to communicate to Gen Y the professional expectations of the company and, yes, you do need to spell out all of the above so that they get it. Also catch them when they are behaving in a professional manner and praise them.

Since Gen Y entered the workforce, conflict over individuality and self-expression has been a major issue for Zoomer management. Gen Ys value self-expression at work more than any generation before them, according to psychologist Nicole Lipkin, who co-authored the book *Y in the Workplace*. "This generation has been taught to express themselves no matter what," she says.

However, Lipkin also says that self-expression through clothes or hair shouldn't overshadow the dress code at work. "The people who are going to be successful are those who respect the culture at the corporation," she says. "In the creative industries, it's a different story, but in more formal industries, there are presentation standards that need to remain in place. It's hard to trust someone who looks like a punk."

Let's look at a Gen Y who refused to change his Mohawk haircut for job interviews. Journalism major Eddie Ebbert, twenty-one, recently sported a Mohawk to his interview for an internship at *Esquire* magazine. His mother had suggested that he get a new, more conventional haircut, but he refused. "If you're not going to hire me because of my hair, I'm not going to work there," he said.

Three interviews later, no one mentioned his hair and he got the position. The first day of his internship, Ebbert, with his Mohawk still intact, showed up in a button-down shirt and pressed pants, following the example of his thirty-five-year-old boss.

Author Rebecca Huntley notes in the book *The World According to Y* that employers have to change management styles to fit the new work ethos. "They are going to have to keep a long leash on Generation Y employees or risk losing them altogether," she writes. Whether or not that means loosening company dress code from "business casual" to "business anything goes" is still uncertain.

Some experts, like Alexandra Levit, author of the book *They Don't Teach Corporate in College*, see a trend towards casual dress. "Regardless of the work environment, I think that Gen Ys are more likely to wear what is actually considered very casual (jeans, tee-shirts) as opposed to the more traditional casual of khakis and button-down shirts," she says.

While Gen Y was just getting comfortable wearing jeans at the office, the recession changed expectations for behavior. "I have seen organizations cracking down on all sorts of behavior that they let slide before because they feel more in control now," says Levit.

The bottom line is to do what works for your team (keeping in mind the predominant generation group) and your industry, but get ready for still more change when the economy improves.

99: Critical Thinking

"The critical habit of thought, if usual in society, will pervade all its mores, because it is a way of taking up the problems of life. Men educated in it cannot be stampeded by stump orators... They are slow to believe. They can hold things as possible or probable in all degrees, without certainty and without pain. They can wait for evidence and weigh evidence, uninfluenced by the emphasis or confidence with which assertions are made on one side or the other. They can resist appeals to their dearest prejudices and all kinds of cajolery. Education in the critical faculty is the only education of which it can be truly said that it makes good citizens. "
> William Graham Sumner, *Folkways*

Just like professionalism or the importance of being on time the skill of critical thinking needs to be taught to Gen Y. Zoomers and Gen X have the advantage of on-the-job experience and many have continued their education by taking leadership courses. Come to think of it, how many of us had to learn critical thinking ourselves?

Some of the key components of critical thinking are:
- ✓ Thinking independently
- ✓ Developing insight into egocentricity or socio-centricity
- ✓ Exercising fair-mindedness
- ✓ Exploring thoughts underlying feelings and feelings underlying thoughts
- ✓ Developing intellectual humility, suspending judgment
- ✓ Developing intellectual courage
- ✓ Developing intellectual good faith or integrity

- ✓ Developing intellectual perseverance
- ✓ Developing confidence in reasoning
- ✓ Refining generalizations and avoiding oversimplifications
- ✓ Comparing analogous situations: transferring insights to new contexts
- ✓ Developing one's perspective: creating or exploring beliefs, arguments or theories
- ✓ Clarifying issues, conclusions or beliefs
- ✓ Clarifying and analyzing the meanings of words or phrases
- ✓ Developing criteria for evaluation: clarifying values and standards
- ✓ Evaluating the credibility of sources of information
- ✓ Questioning deeply: raising and pursuing root or significant questions
- ✓ Analyzing or evaluating arguments, interpretations, beliefs or theories
- ✓ Generating or assessing solutions
- ✓ Listening critically: the art of silent dialogue
- ✓ Making interdisciplinary connections
- ✓ Noting significant similarities and differences
- ✓ Examining or evaluating assumptions
- ✓ Recognizing contradictions
- ✓ Exploring implications and consequences.

When you read this list you can see that some of these skills are developed with experience and over time. If you were to rate yourself on the list above I am sure you would find there are areas of critical thinking that you could personally improve upon. Use this list as a training tool when coaching your team—critical thinking is a huge asset. When coached or taught to your Gen X and Gen Ys (and Zoomers for that matter) you increase your competitive advantage.

100: Stress Management

Of course all of us need to practice stress management regardless of our generation. The stresses of today include ongoing change, increased technology and increasingly complex business relationships (such as culture and global business). What causes stress is unique to us as individuals but perception plays a key role in how we manage our stress.

Mihaly Csikszentmihalyi is the author of *Flow*. He suggests that stress is a good thing when it is positive. He believes that when we are in the flow of our work or doing something we enjoy there is tension but in the tension there is joy and pleasure. The opposite of positive stress is negative stress, where we perceive that time is our enemy, or that other people or situations are to blame for our stressful situations.

It stands to reason that if we are building a workplace where all of the generations are happy that lower levels of stress and more episodes of flow would occur. Some companies offer on-site massage for their employees, or a quiet room where employees can sit and read, listen to their iPods or even close their eyes for a bit. And other companies are offering meditation programs right at people's desks so that they can participate in deep breathing and imagery exercises to help them release tension.

I took a look at what might cause negative stress for each of the generations and here is what my research indicated:

Gen Y: being unhappy at work, going to school while working

Gen X: trying to balance work and family, workloads, PDAs and 24–7 availability

Zoomers: having teenagers and elderly parents to care for in addition to heavy workloads.

As leaders we need to coach our teams to manage stress. Often the stress is self-created and all that is required is a new way of dealing with the challenge. For example, I had a client I was coaching who was a Gen X—she was intensely stressed and her demeanor was quite abrupt. It turned out she had quit smoking about two months prior and she wasn't managing well. When I suggested to her that she get support from her naturopath to help her, she tried acupuncture and it made a notable difference.

I am not going to go into the usual prescription for stress management because I feel that a lot of people aren't going to do what's suggested anyway. For example, meditation can seem too daunting for a stressed person. Instead I recommend listening to meditation audios. Companies that offer exercise on site see a dramatic difference in employees' ability to manage their stress, as well.

It goes back to companies and leaders caring about reducing stress for their employees and taking care of their own stress levels. And of course the more we focus on providing work that people love, the more they will be experiencing positive stress, or flow.

101: The Future of Work

Flash-forward to ten years from now—the year 2020—and what do you think the workplace will look like? I predict the way we work will be drastically different and I believe that work will be a more organic part of our lives. Here are some of my predictions for the future of work looking ahead to the year 2020:

- ✓ New employees will be able to choose to work in the head office, in a regional satellite office or from home.
- ✓ Companies will do personality and work choice alignment tests prior to hiring to ensure the employees' strengths are a match for the work.
- ✓ Companies will offer all of the perks of working from home or at the head office location with working "pods" similar to what you see in the new Boeing 737 airplanes. Employees can put their feet up while working on their computers.
- ✓ Computers will be like the ones we see in movies and on TV. They will be translucent boards where data can be moved around with a swipe, a touch and a tap, very similar to iPhones and touch PDAs.
- ✓ Virtual office meetings will be in holographic format—a presenter can be holographically projected into a meeting area and it is as if they are there in person. The audience can interact as if they were there.
- ✓ Visors will come down from the earpiece of Bluetooth phones to allow you to read a document as if it were full size, anywhere in the world.

- ✓ Talking to computers will become much more common. A team working on a project will be able to verbalize their ideas and the computer will immediately use the data from the verbal information to calculate and show a variety of possible forecast scenarios.
- ✓ Health will be a key determinant to success in a company. Employees who take superior care of themselves will earn points, prizes and special recognition.
- ✓ Project work will be the new norm—work won't be for five or ten-year cycles but for one or two-year contracts. Because companies will be focused on "pay for performance," contract renewal will be based on results.
- ✓ Global conferences will allow people of all cultures to gather and completely understand each other's language. Instead of typical translation methods each participant will wear a device in the ear that will automatically translate into your language whatever the speaker is saying.
- ✓ Transparency will be completely normal. Companies will openly disclose their profits and losses and their employee programs online. There will no longer be secret information. Employees can "out" issues instantly in an online forum.

I believe the world of work will be greatly affected by new technology and to get there we need to be able to make Generations X, Y and Zoomers happy at work.

About the Author

Cheryl Cran is a leadership and generations in the workplace expert. She has worked with corporations such as McDonalds, AstraZeneca, 3M, Giant Foods, Big Lots, Growmark and many more. As a consultant, Cheryl has helped organizations with their leadership and people development, which has increased productivity, profitability and happiness at work.

For more than fifteen years Cheryl has worked as a consultant. Her research has been presented at numerous conferences across North America. She is the author of the bestselling books *The Control Freak Revolution* and *50 Ways to Lead & Love It*.

Cheryl has been a guest expert and presented for the TED talks at TEDx Vancouver (www.ted.com). Frequently in the media, she has been on Fox TV and Shaw TV, and has been interviewed on more than 100 radio shows. She is often quoted in the media on issues regarding leadership and generations in the workplace.

To find out more about Cheryl's articles, free e-books and more, please visit www.cherylcran.com . You can e-mail Cheryl's office at info@cherylcran.com .

To book Cheryl to speak at your next event
please call 1 877 307 7403
or e-mail cherylbookings@cmispeakers.com

INDEX